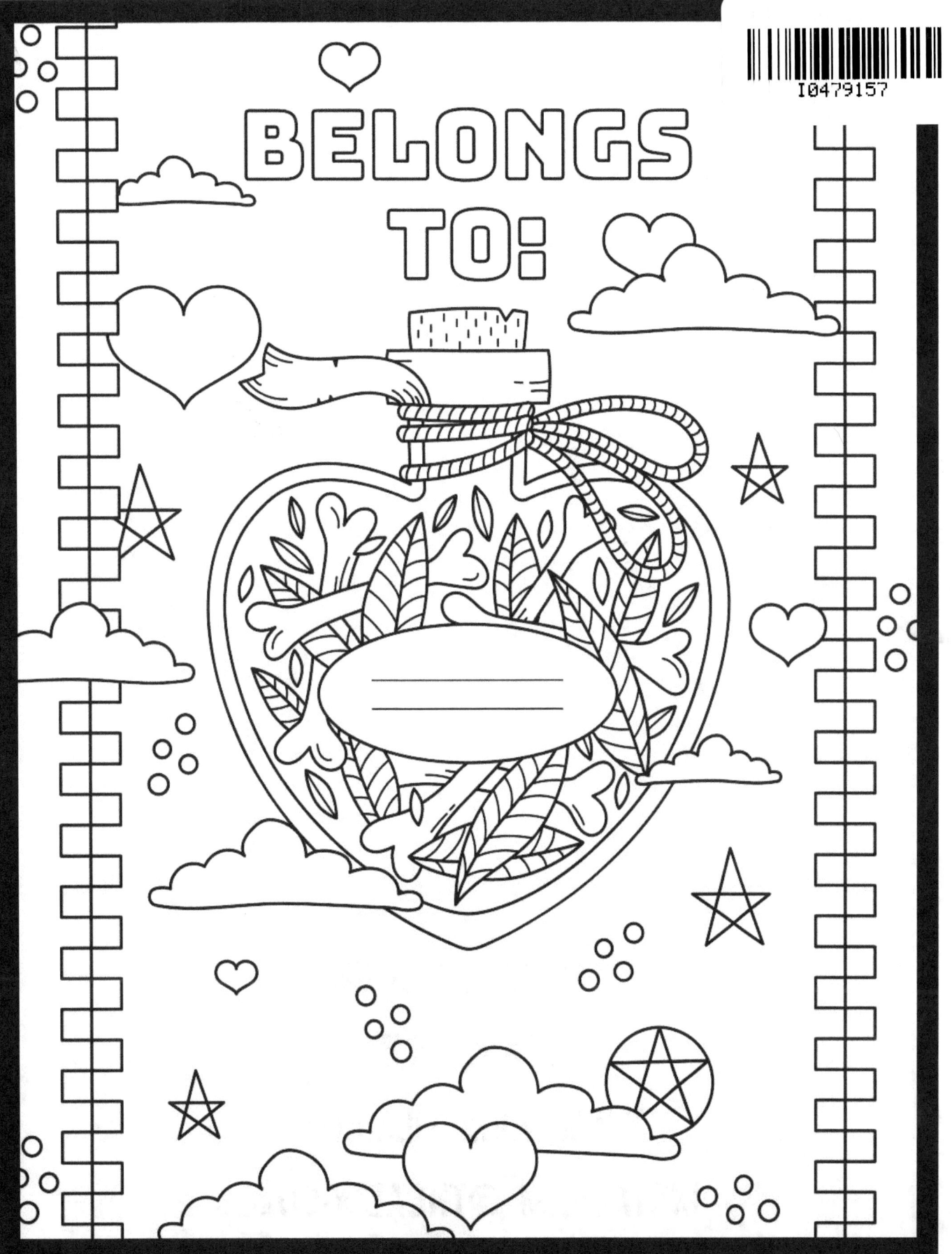

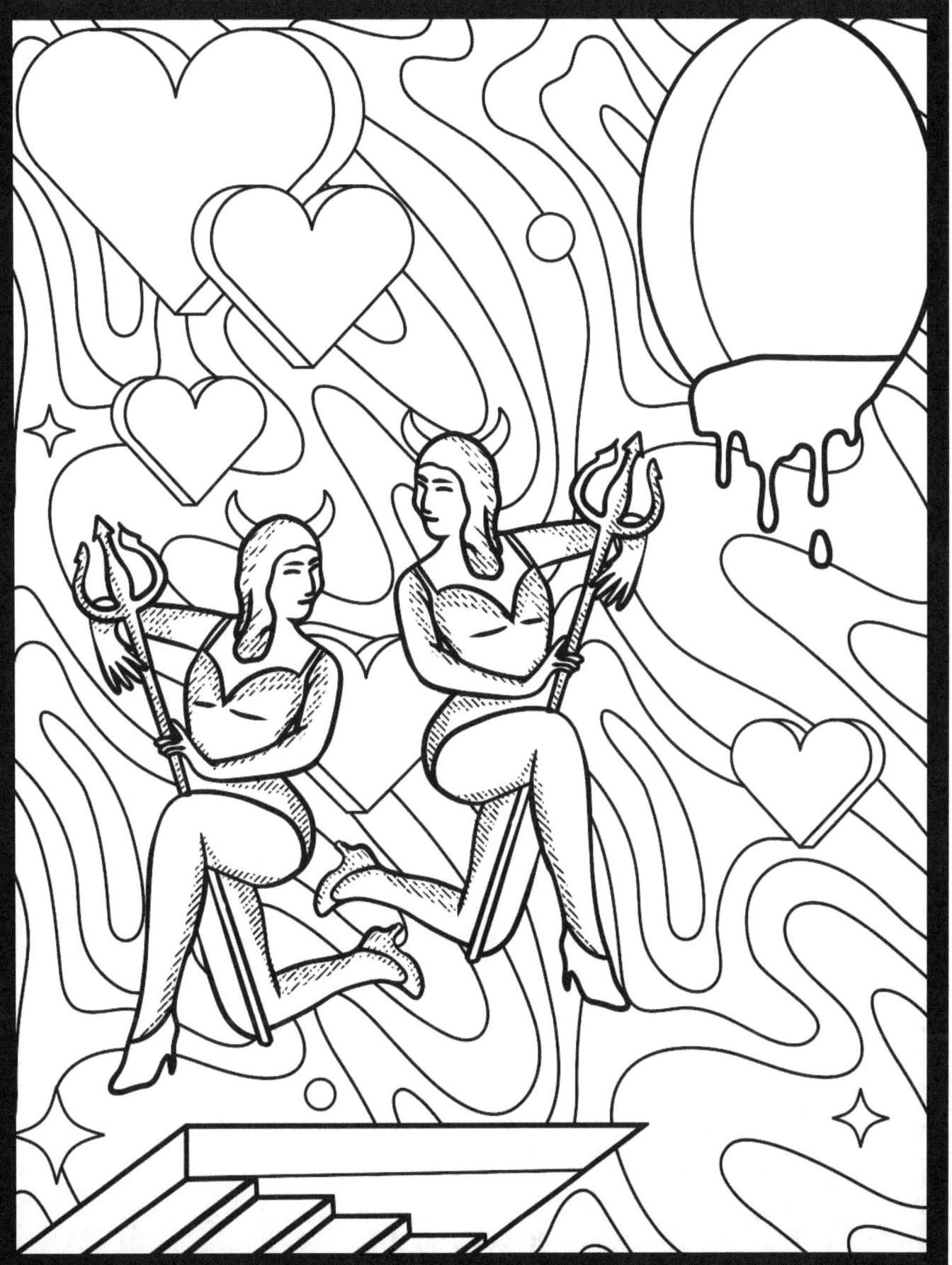

WELCOME

LOVE YOURSELF FIRST THOUGH

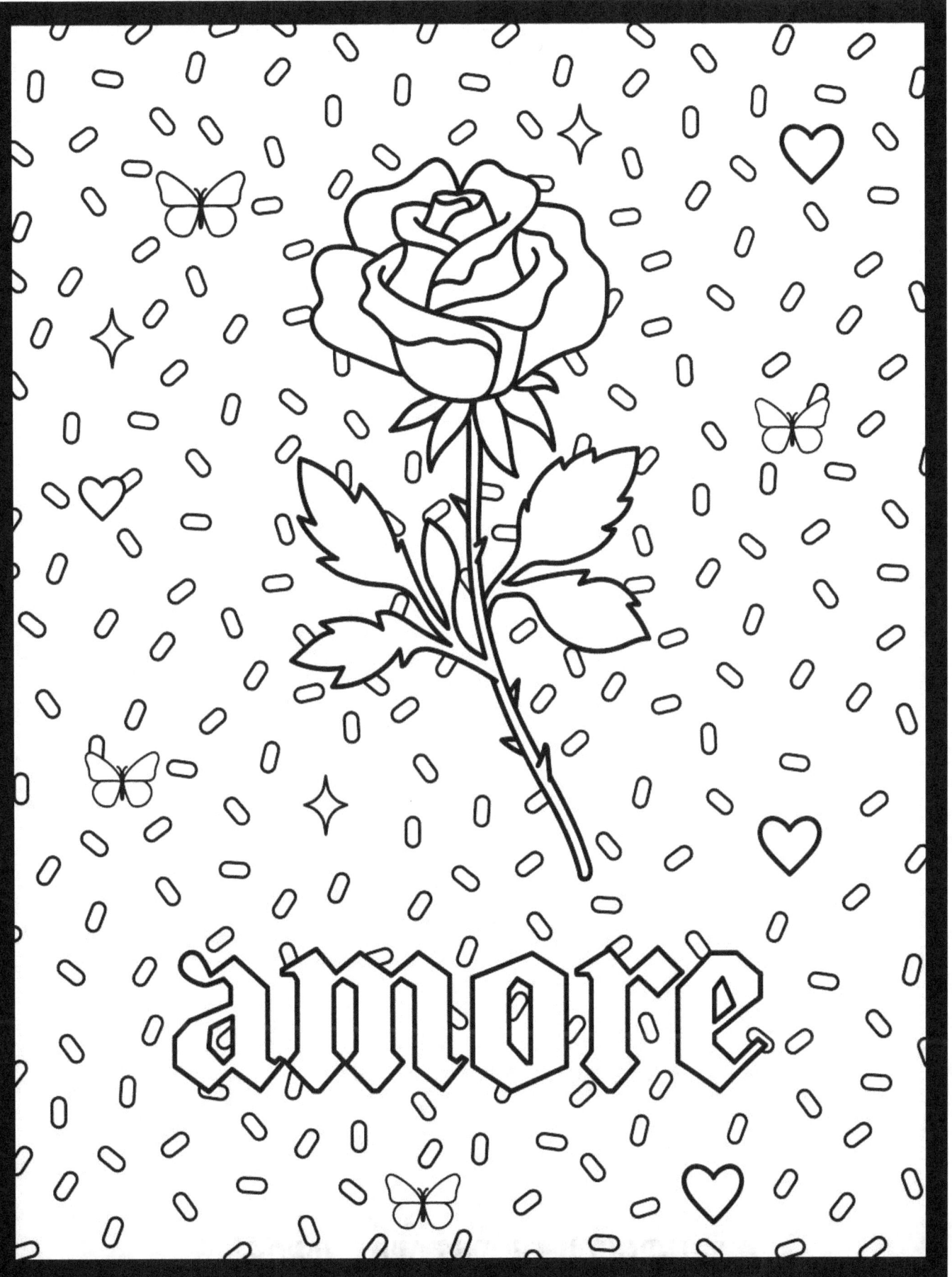

THROUGH THORNS AND CHANGE

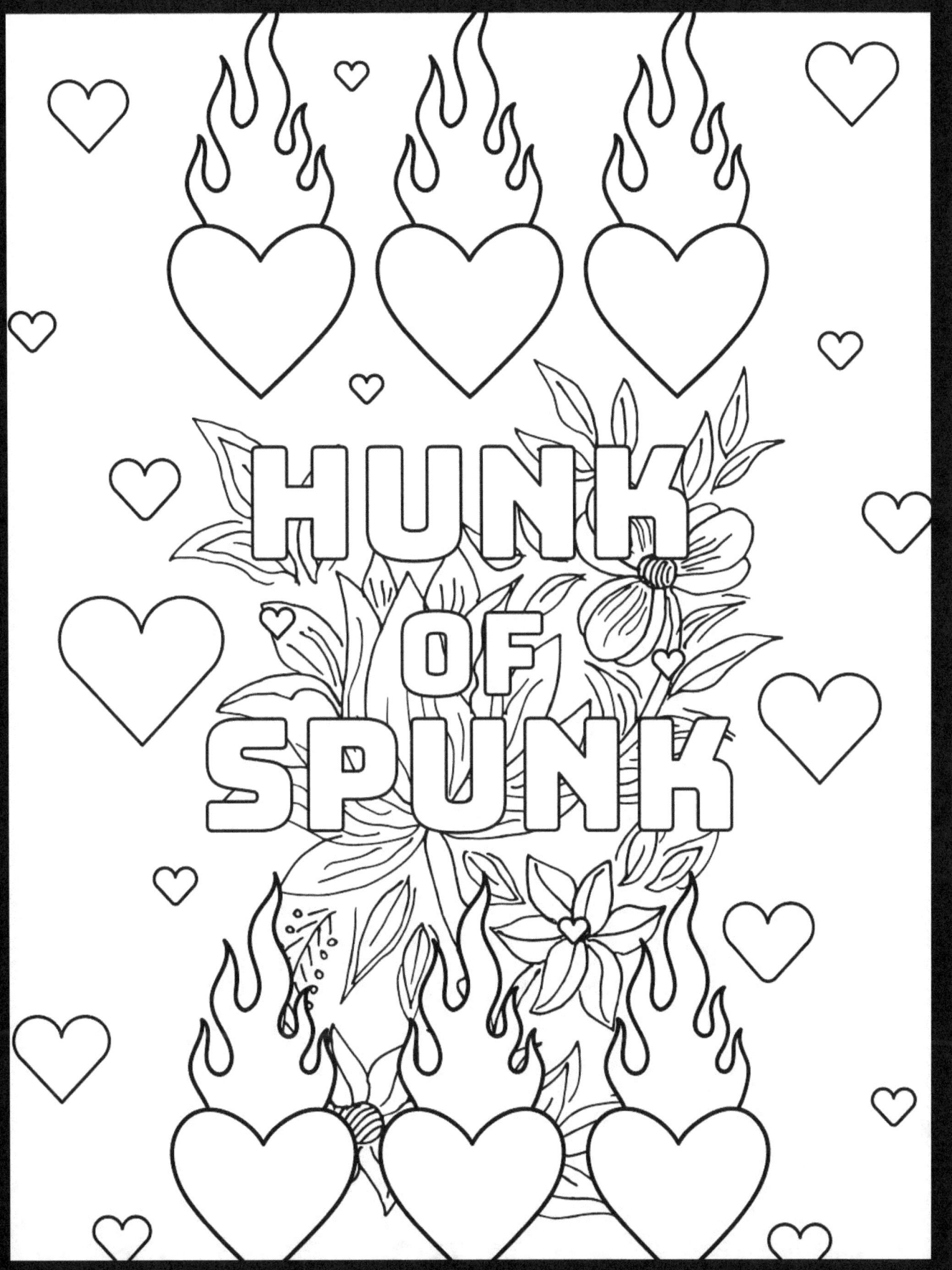

FACTS

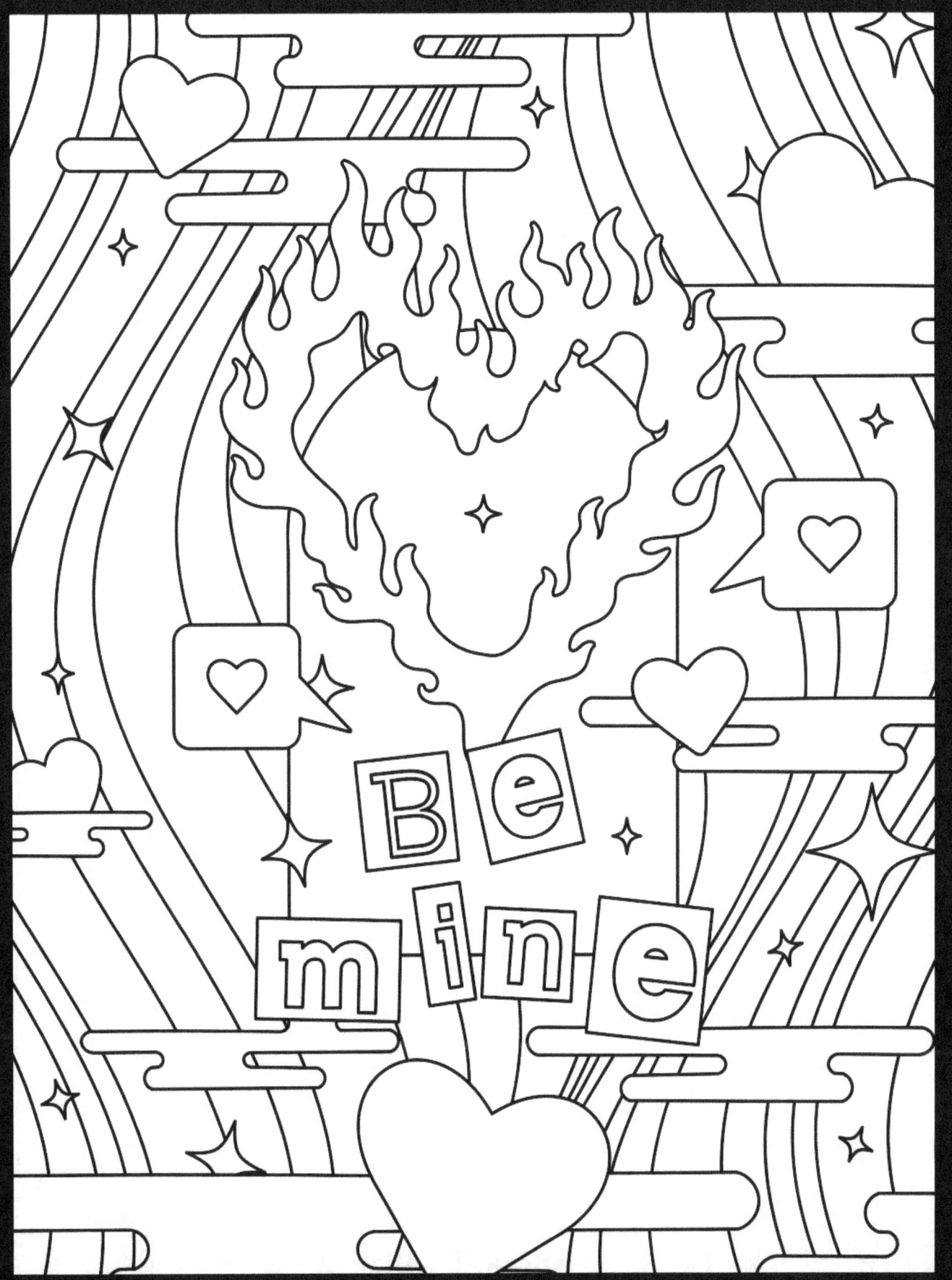

NUMBER ONE

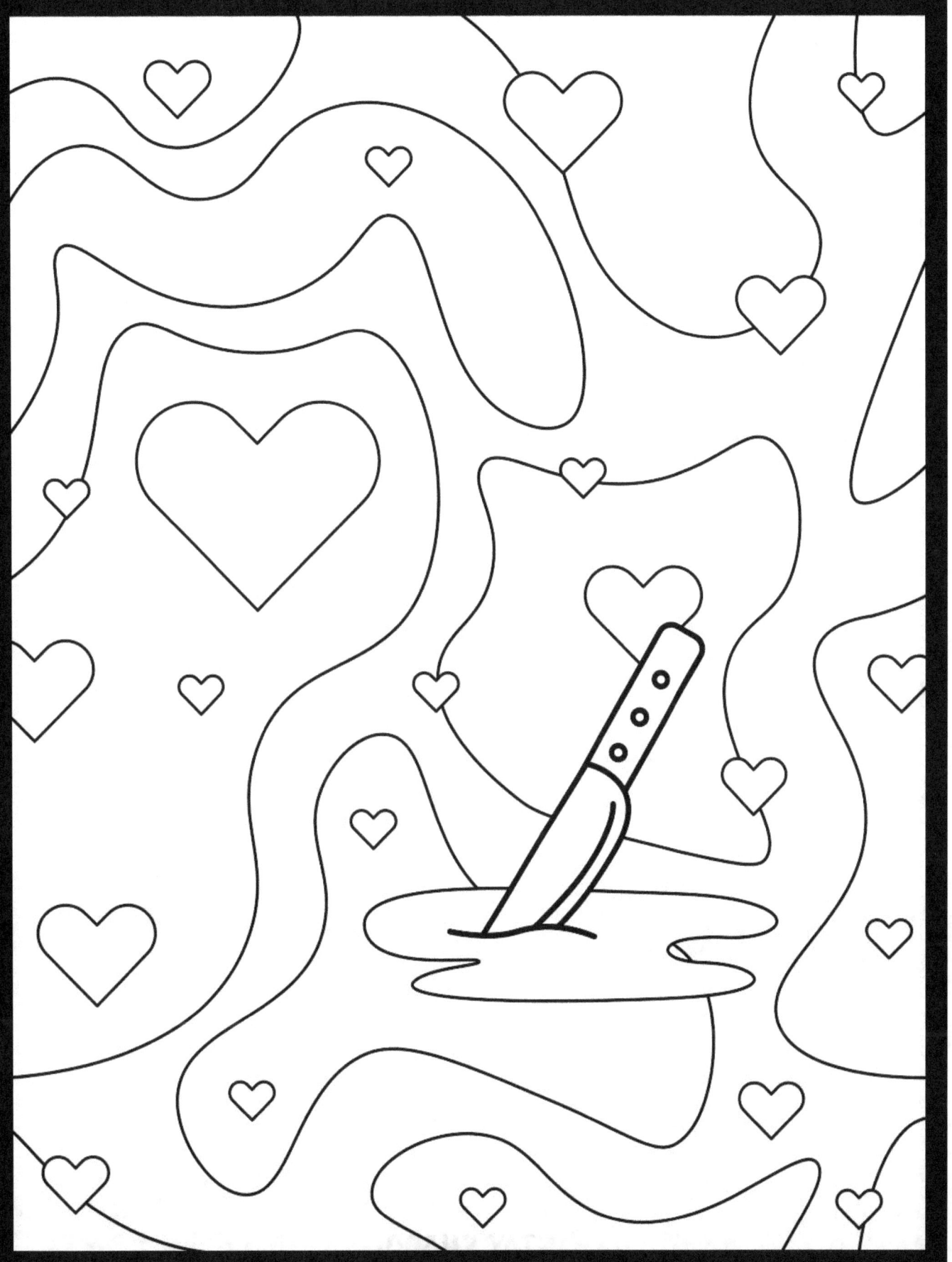

STAY SHARP

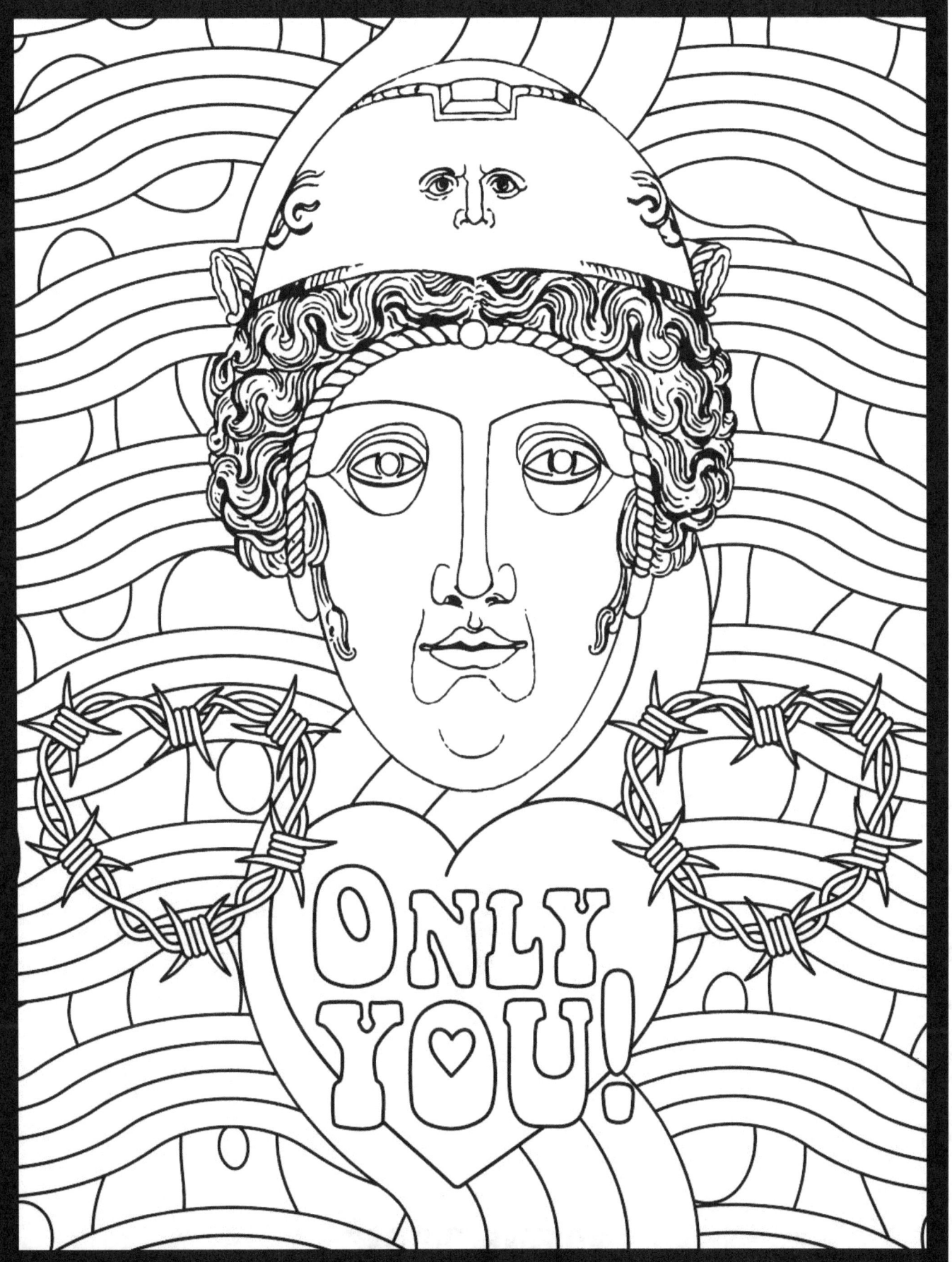

YOU ARE THE ONE

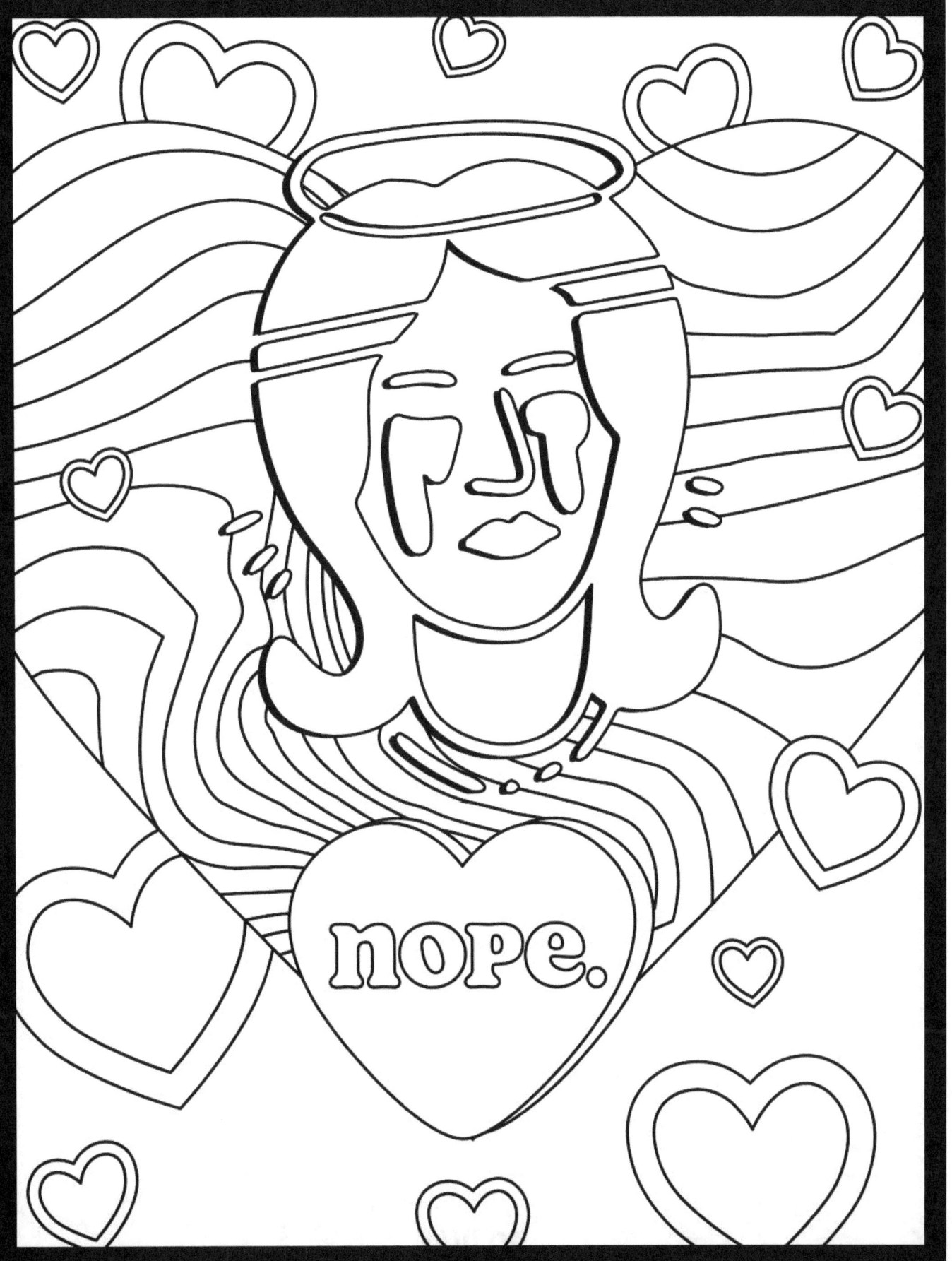

NO WAY

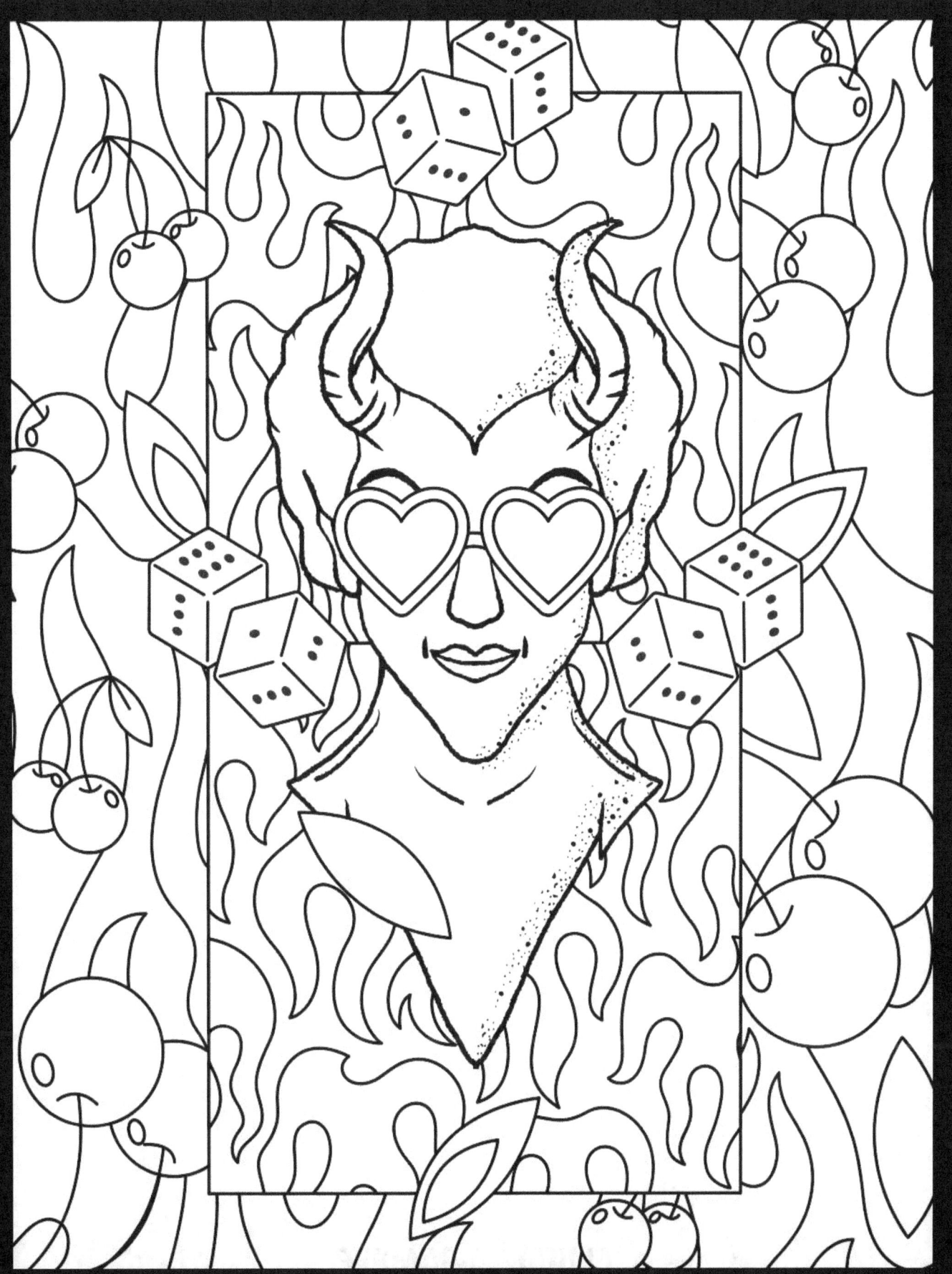

ALWAYS A GAMBLE

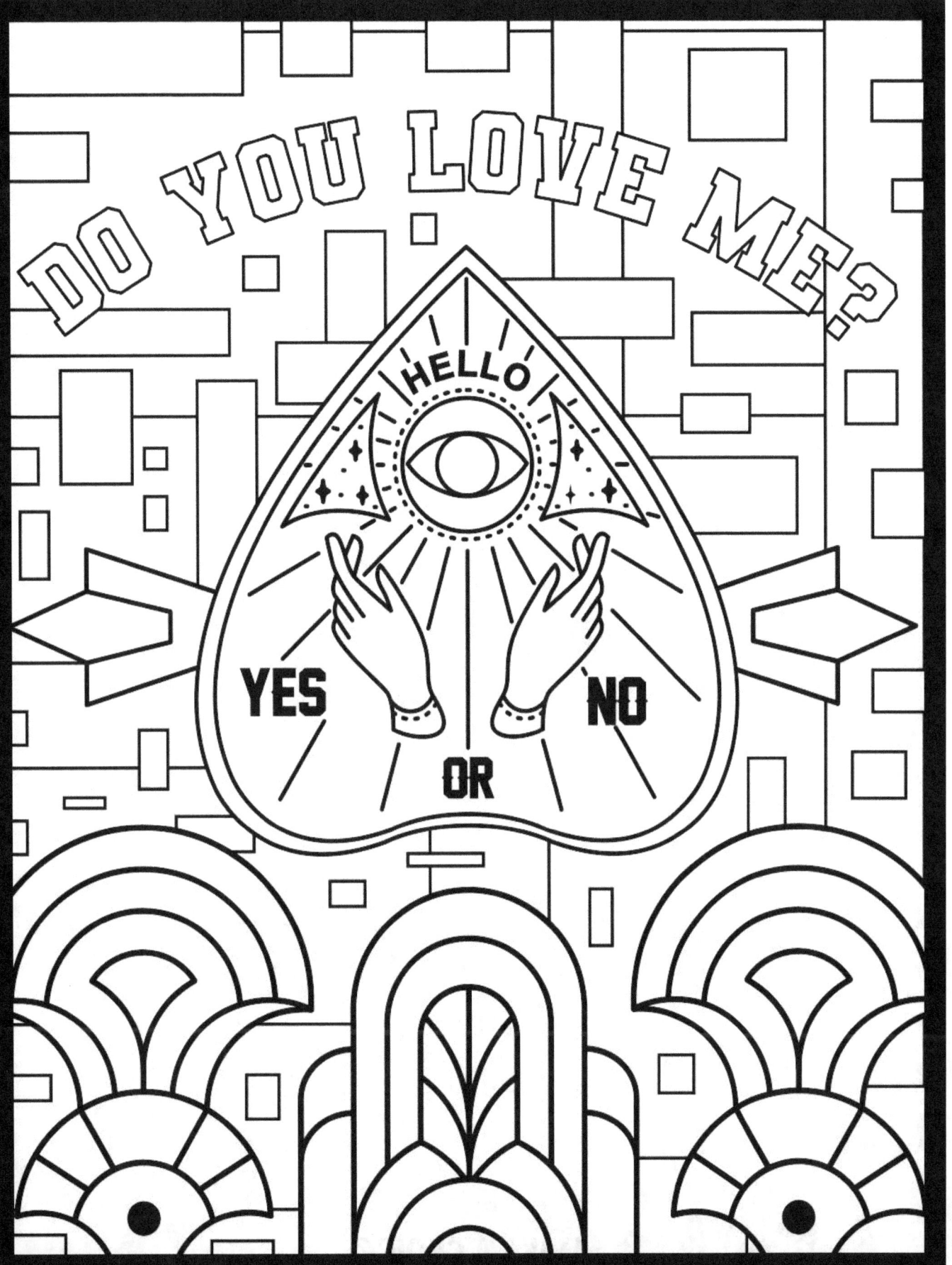

MAKE A CHOICE

POUR IT ALL OUT

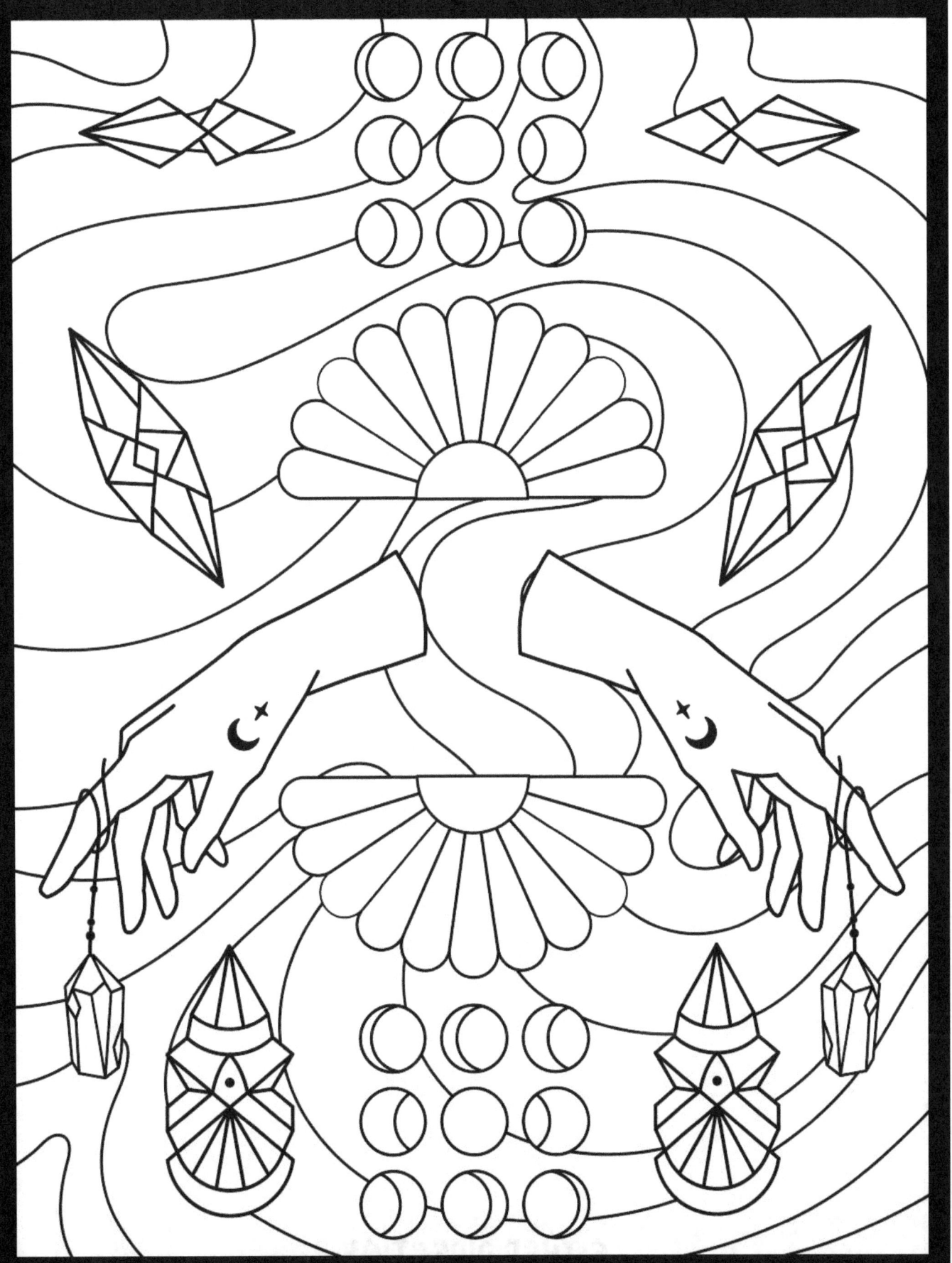

EITHER DIRECTION

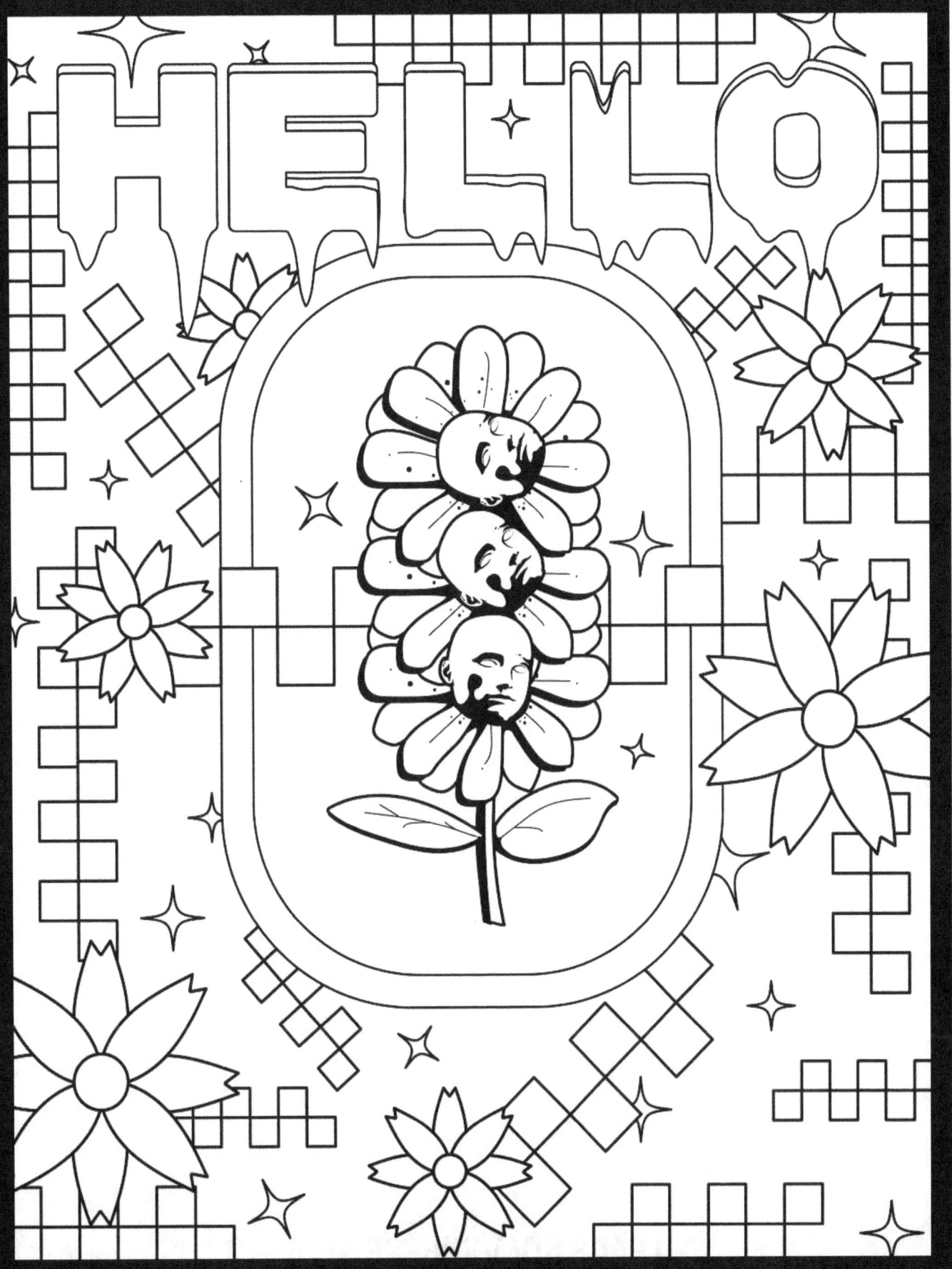

LEADS SOMEWHERE NEW

SOARING

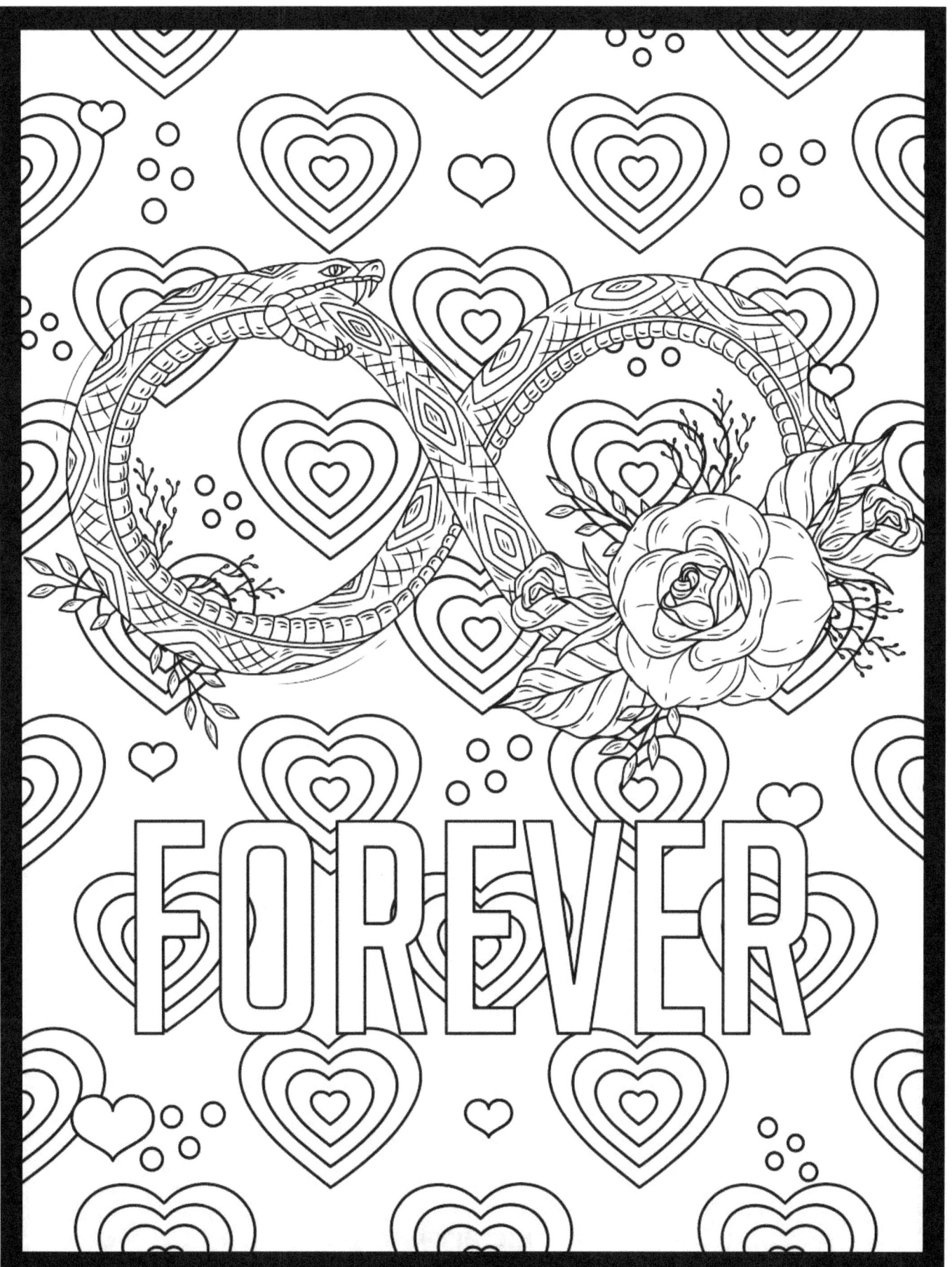

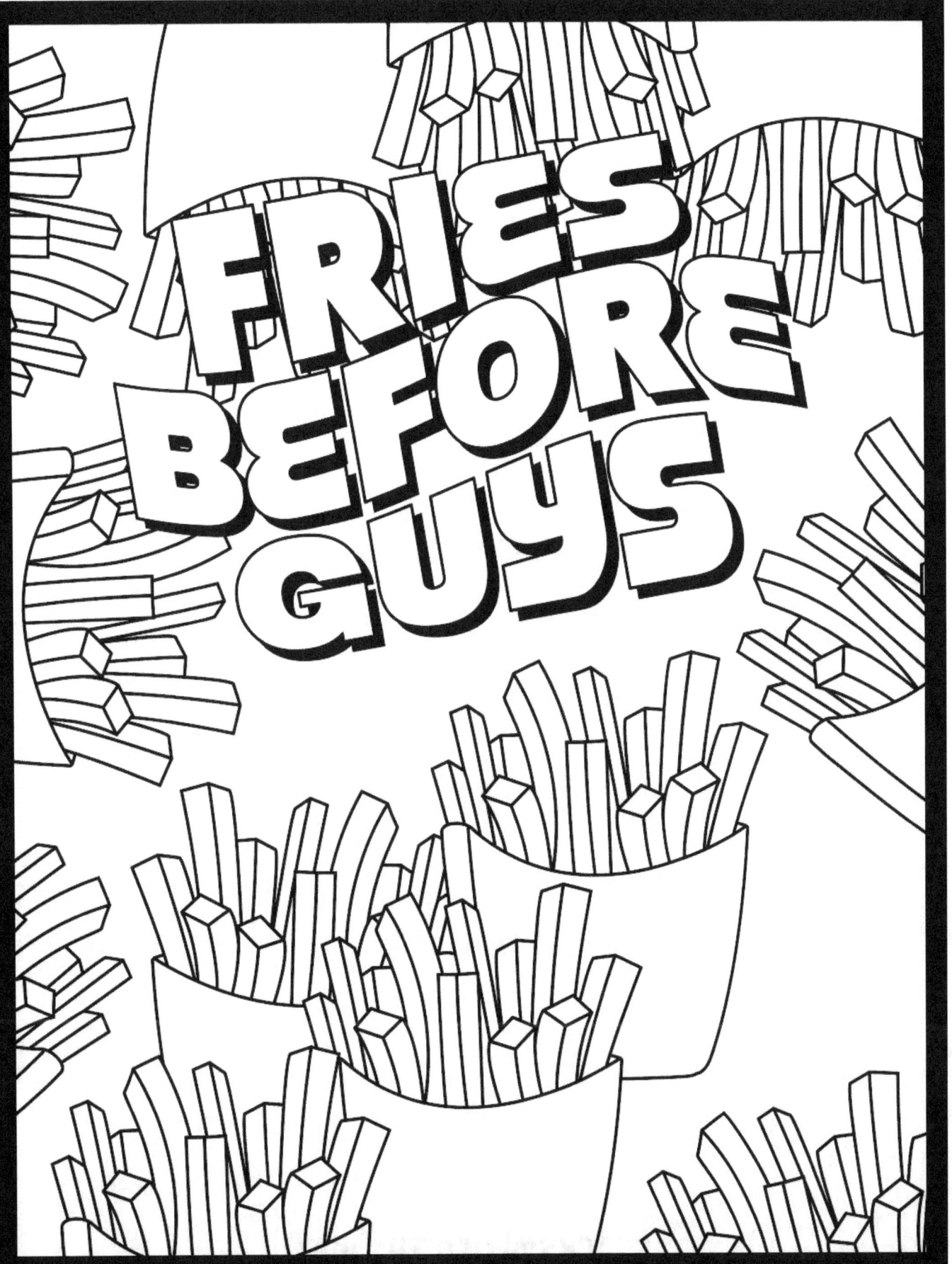

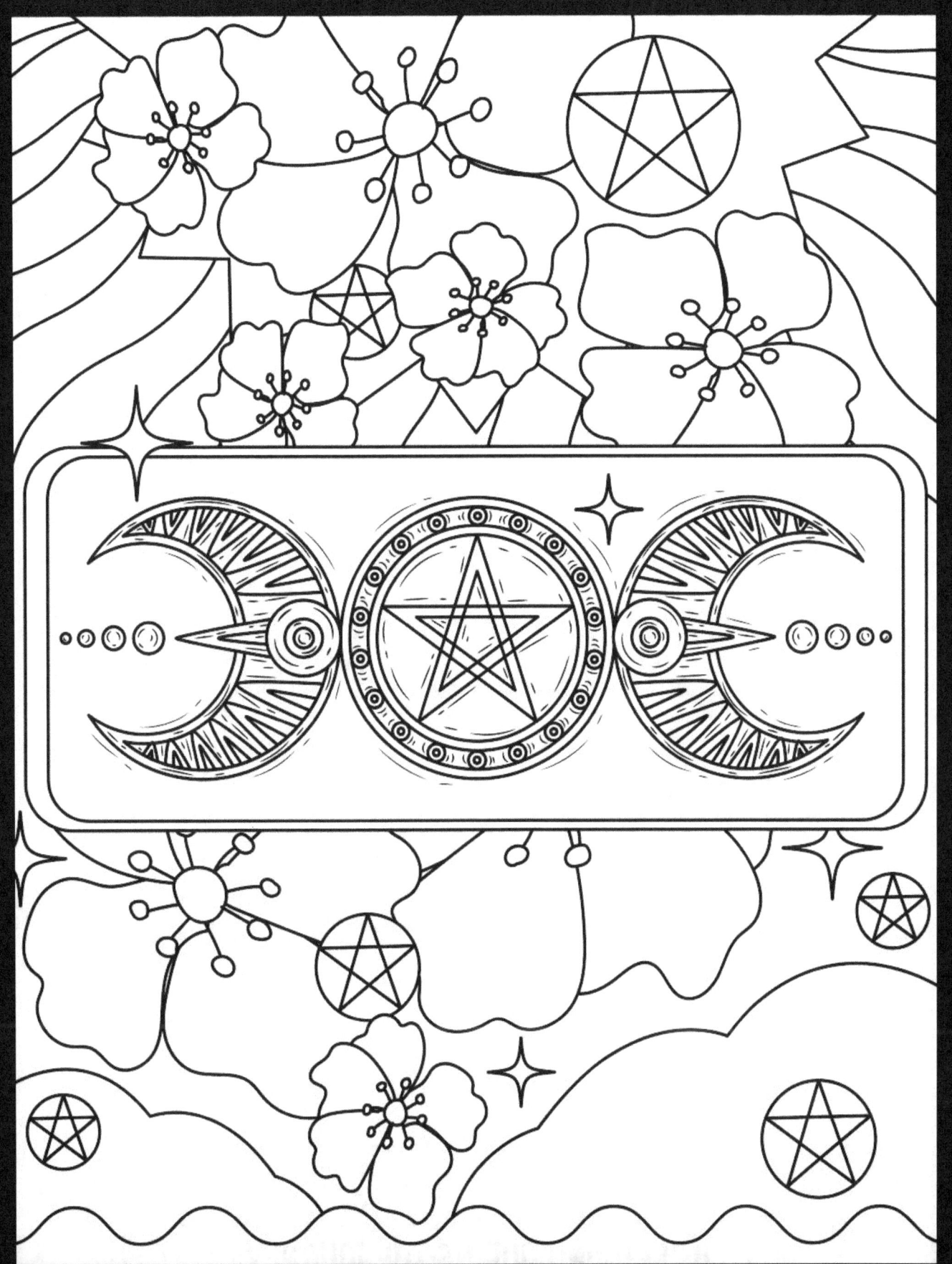

DESERVING DURING THE JOURNEY

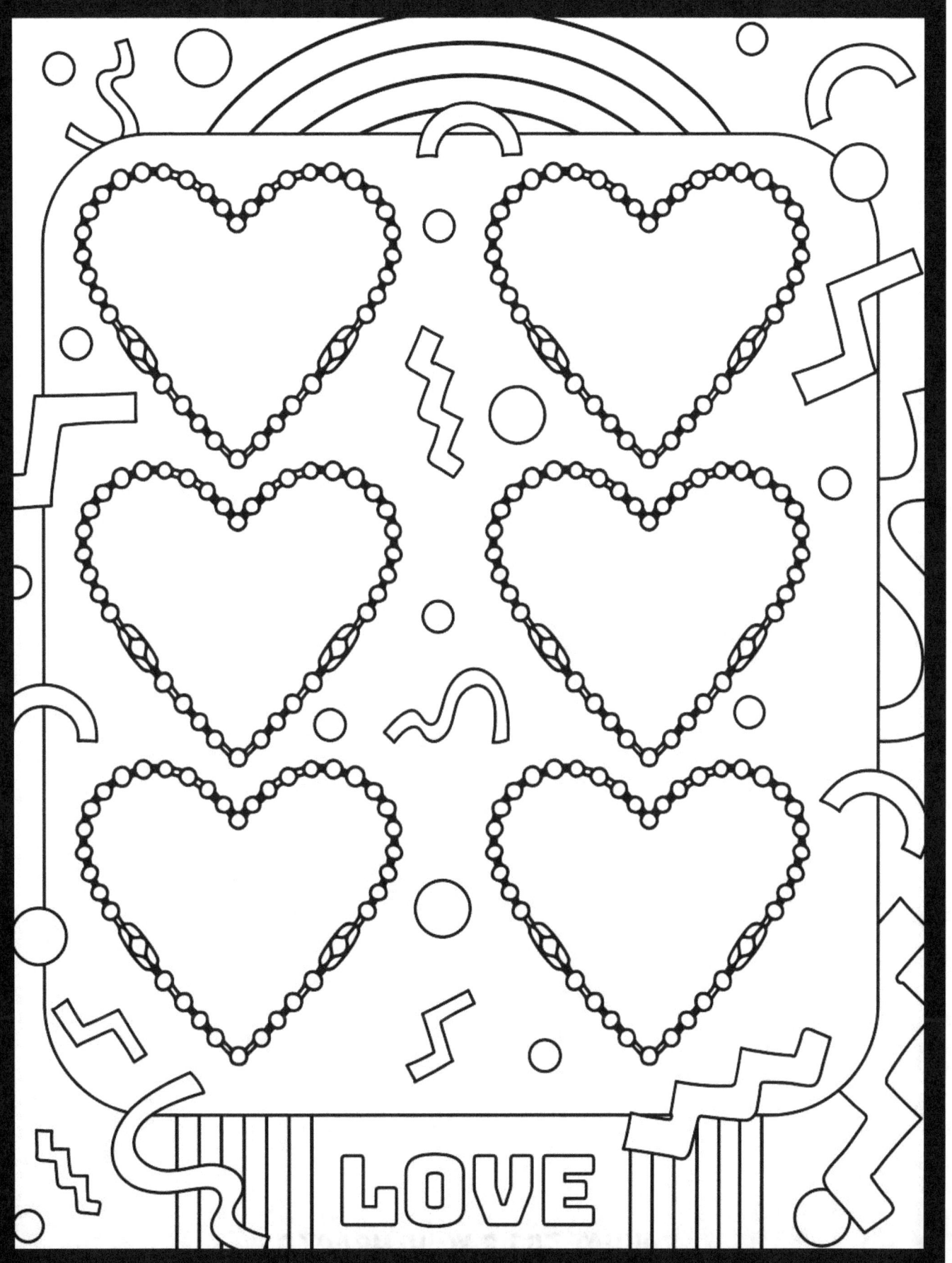

WHAT FILLS YOUR HEART?

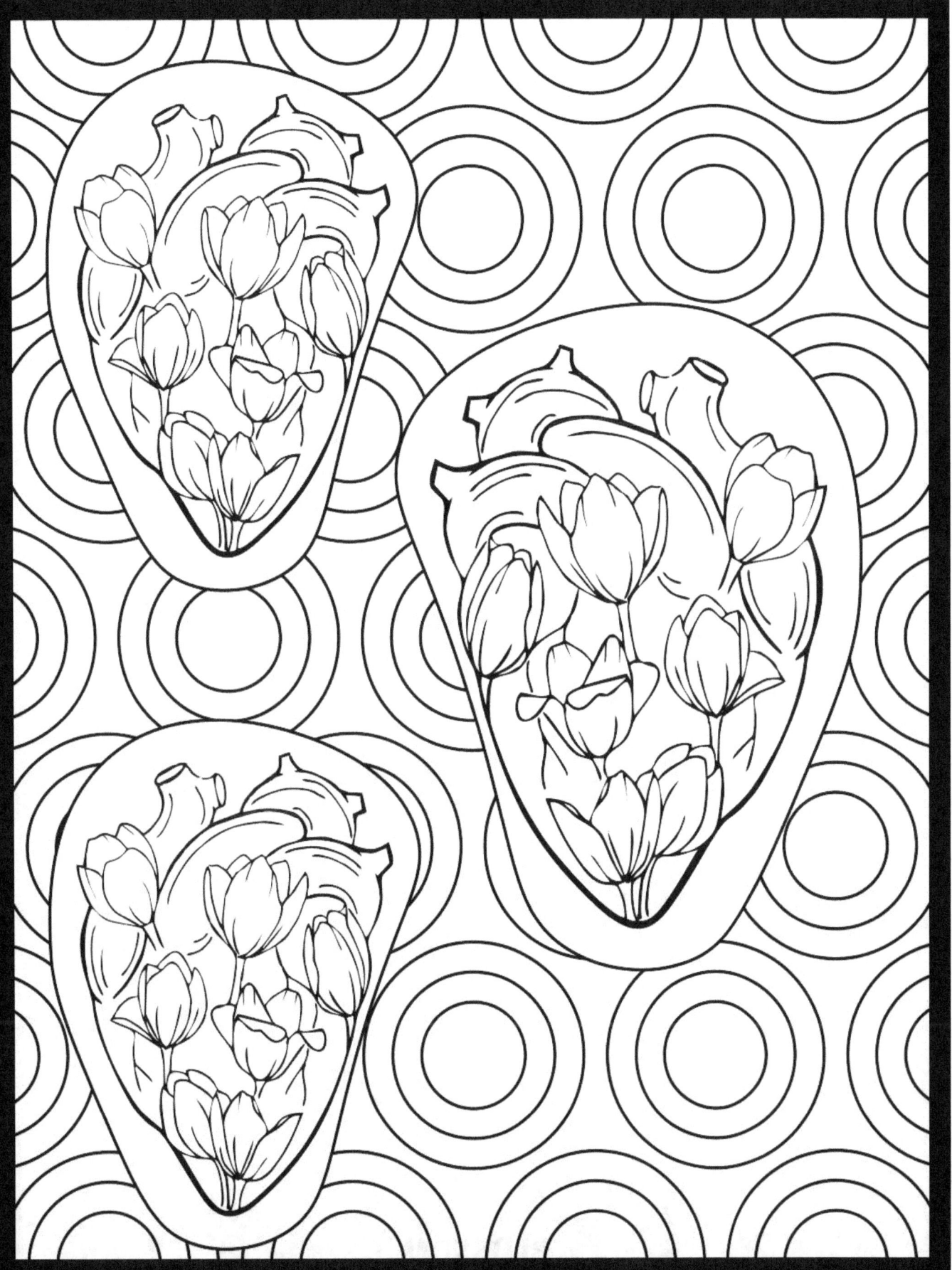

BLOSSOM

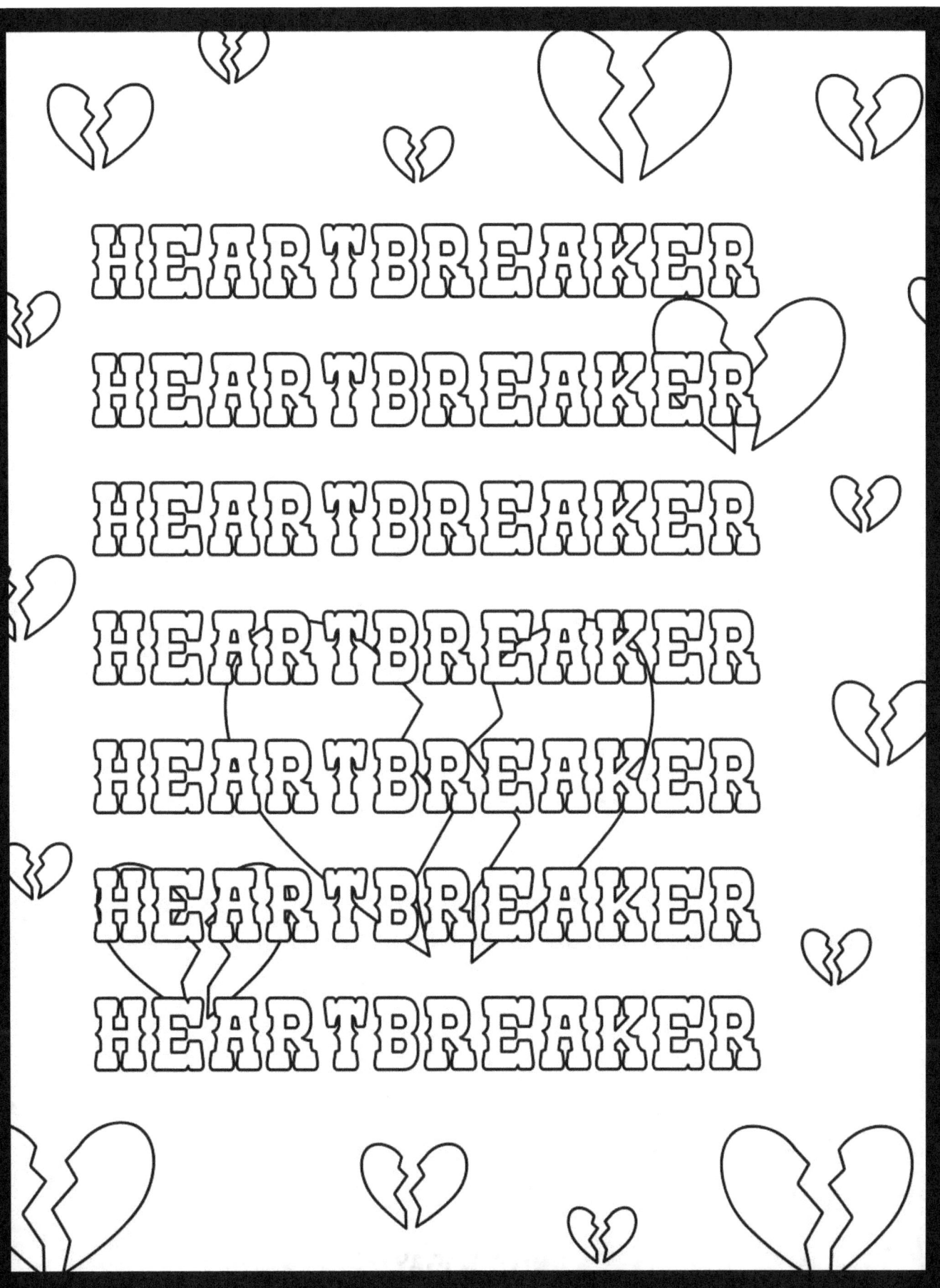

NOT TODAY

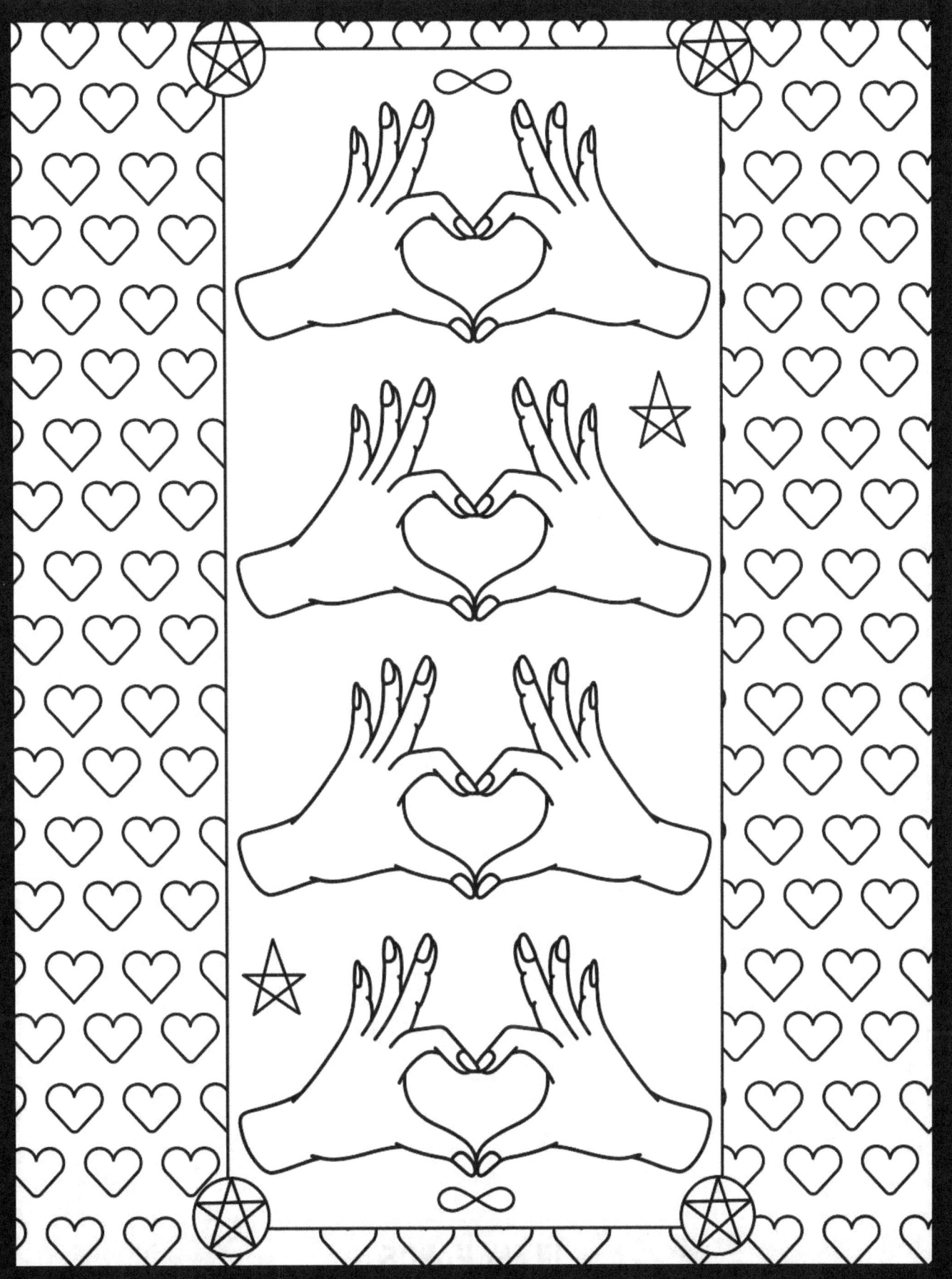

IN MY HANDS

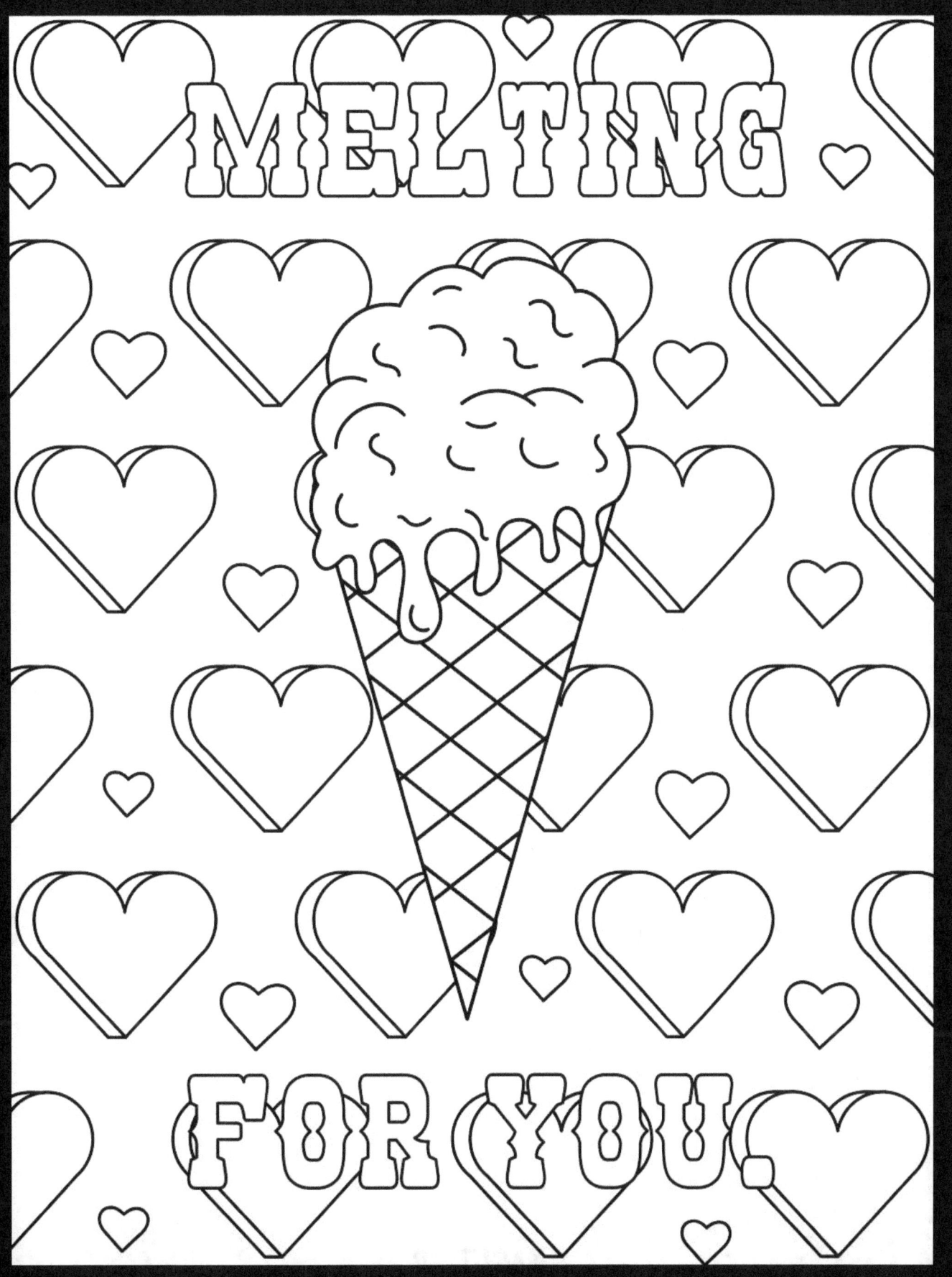

MELTING

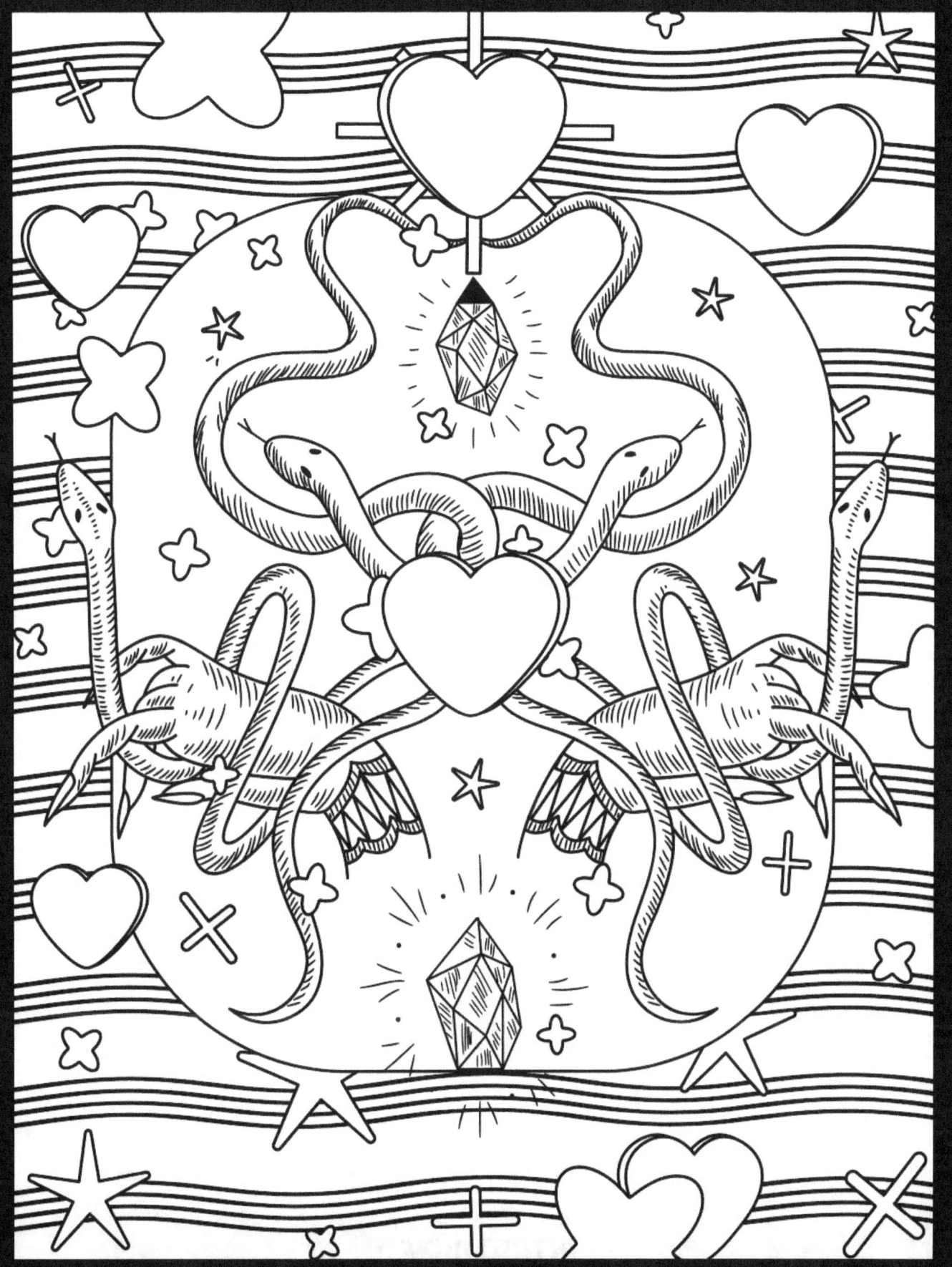

INTERTWINED

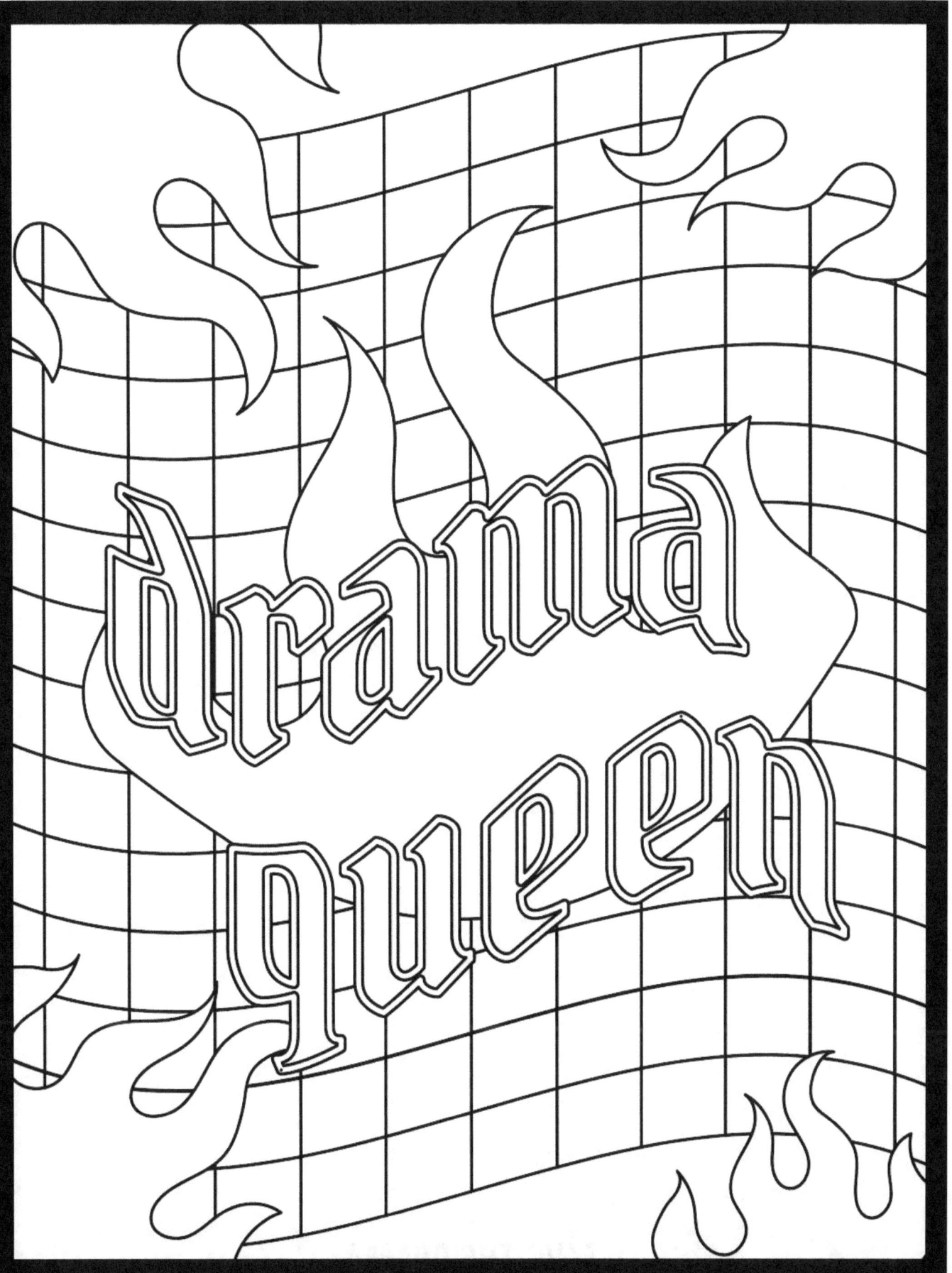

SAVE THE DRAMA

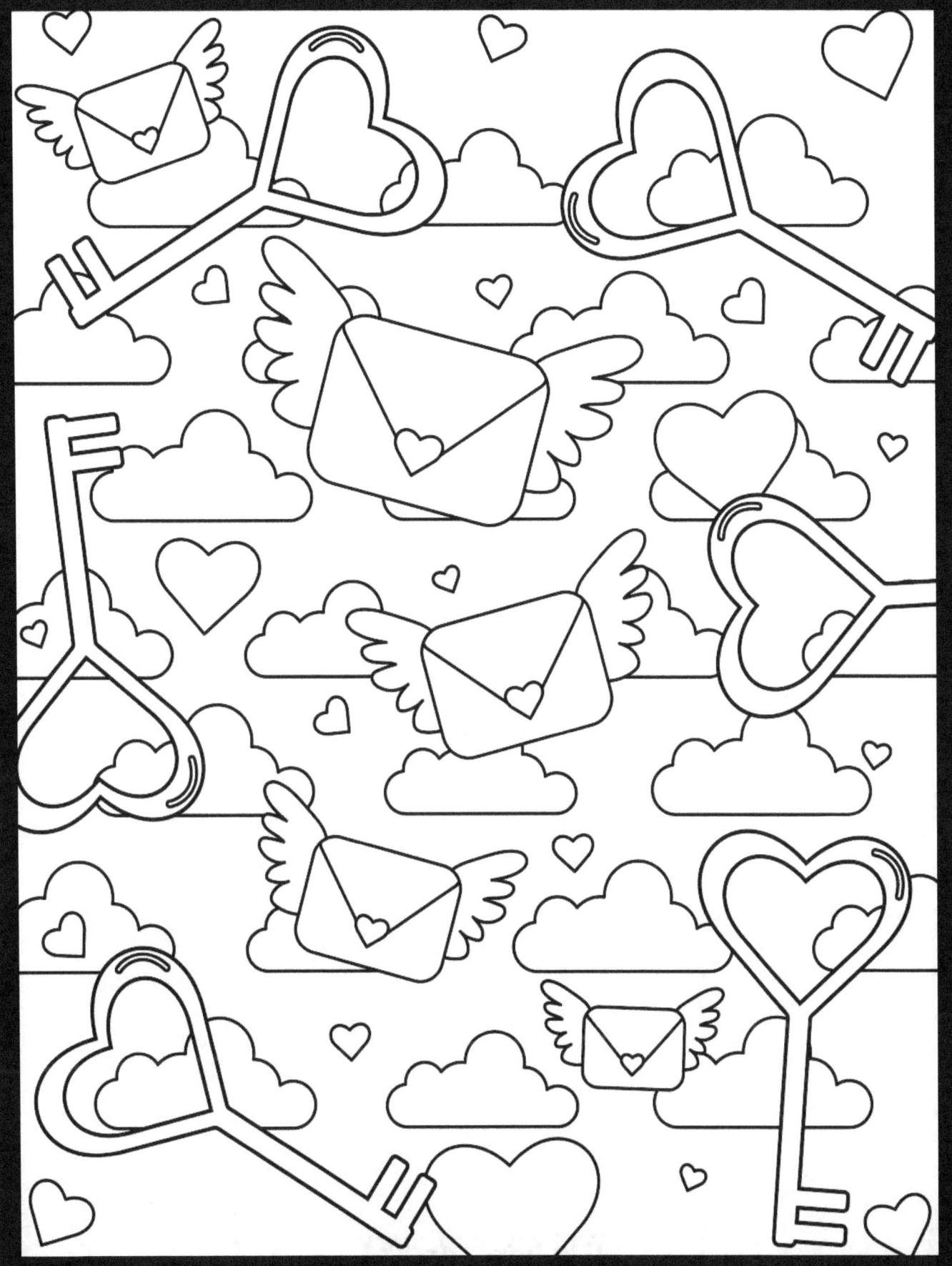

YOU ARE THE KEY

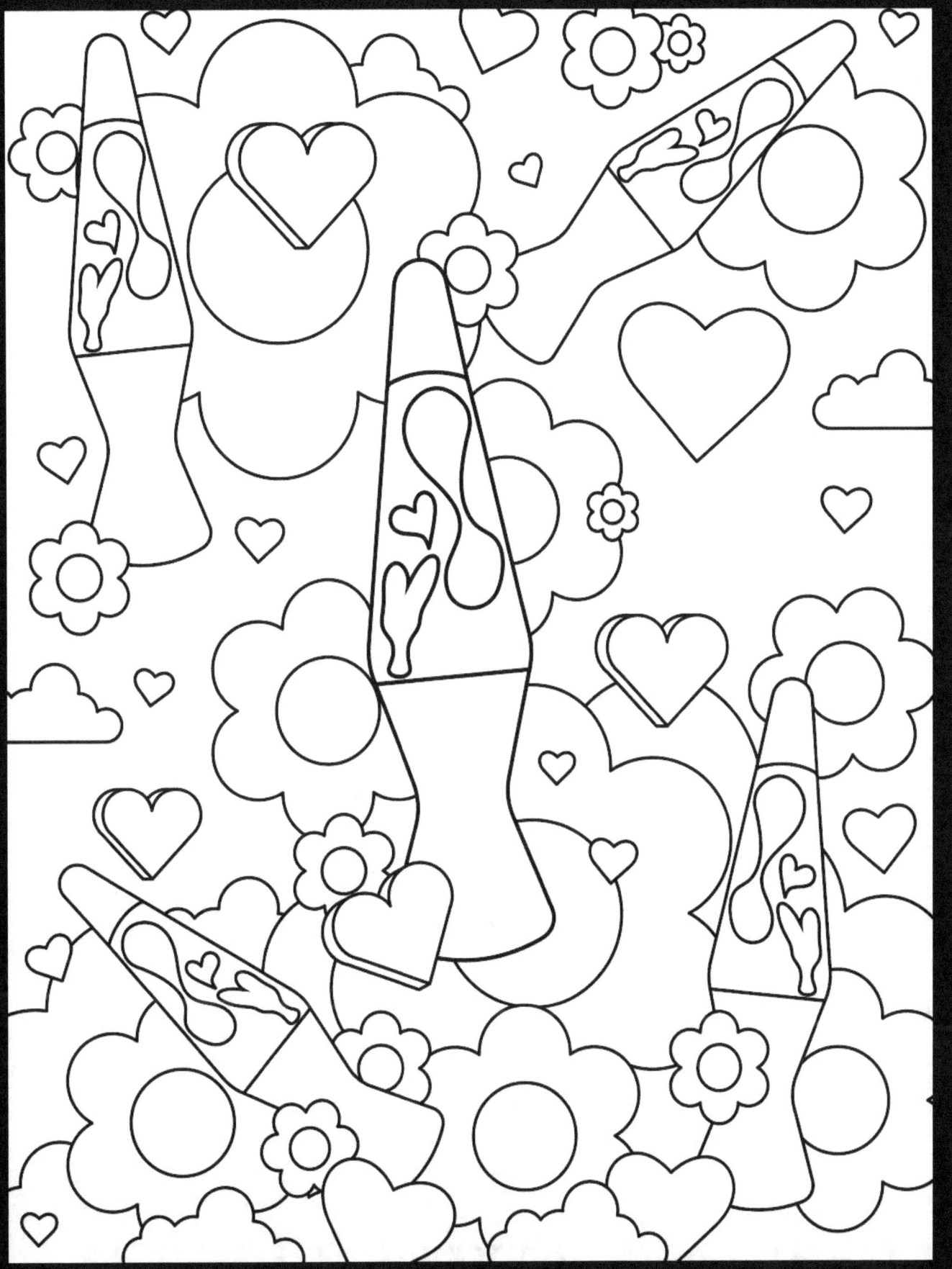

MOLTEN HOT

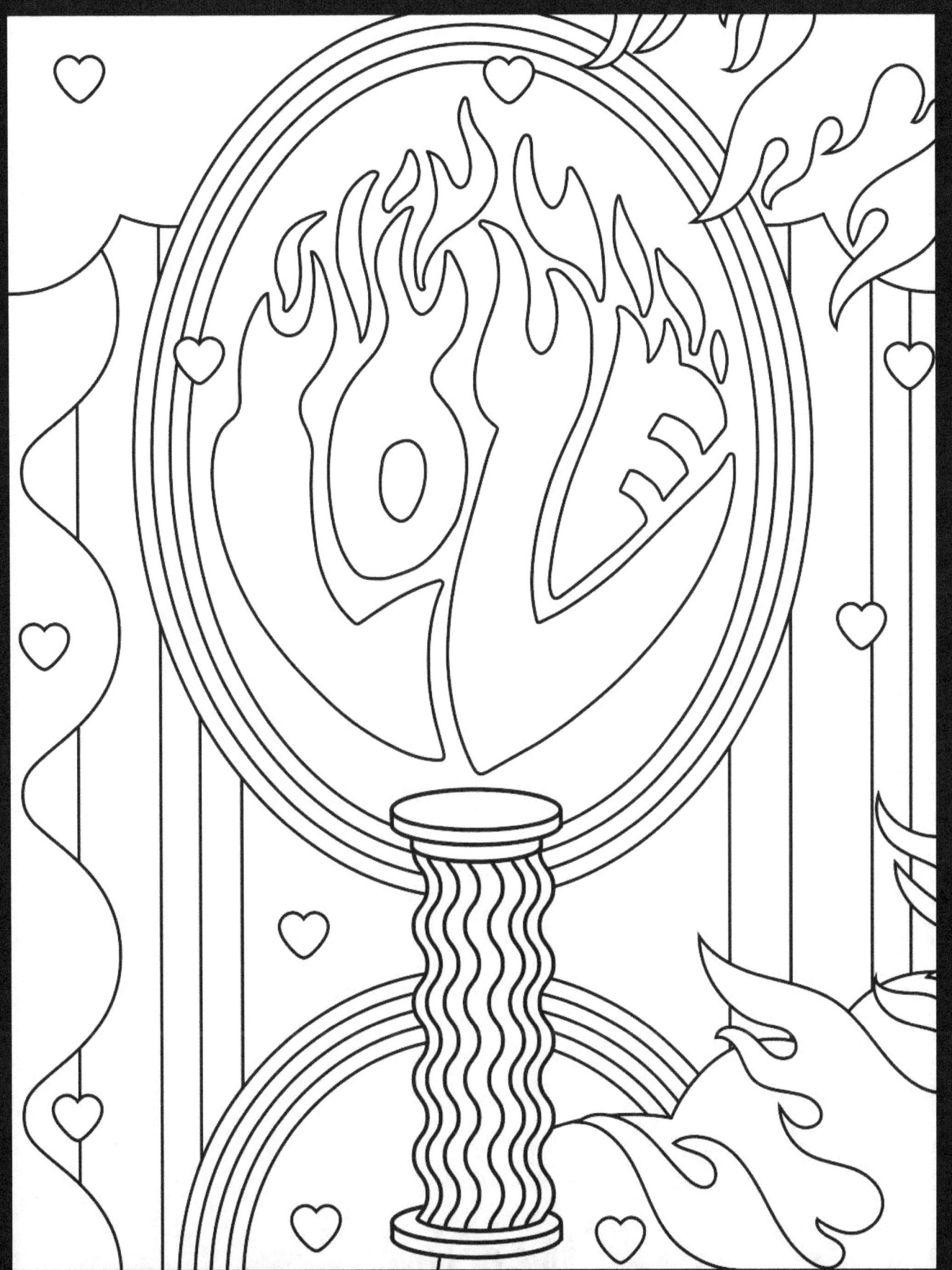

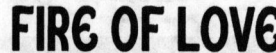
FIRE OF LOVE

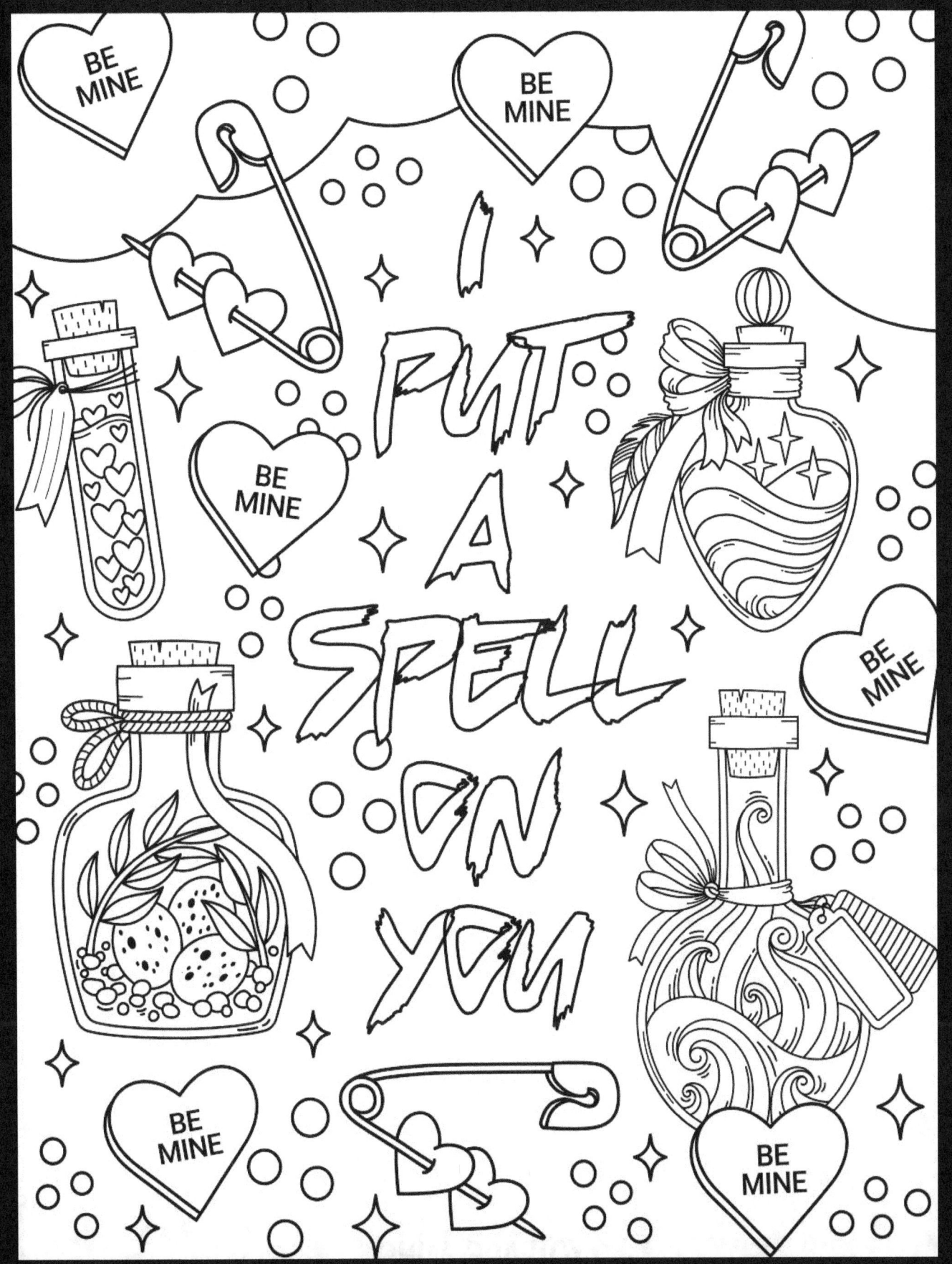

YOU ARE MINE

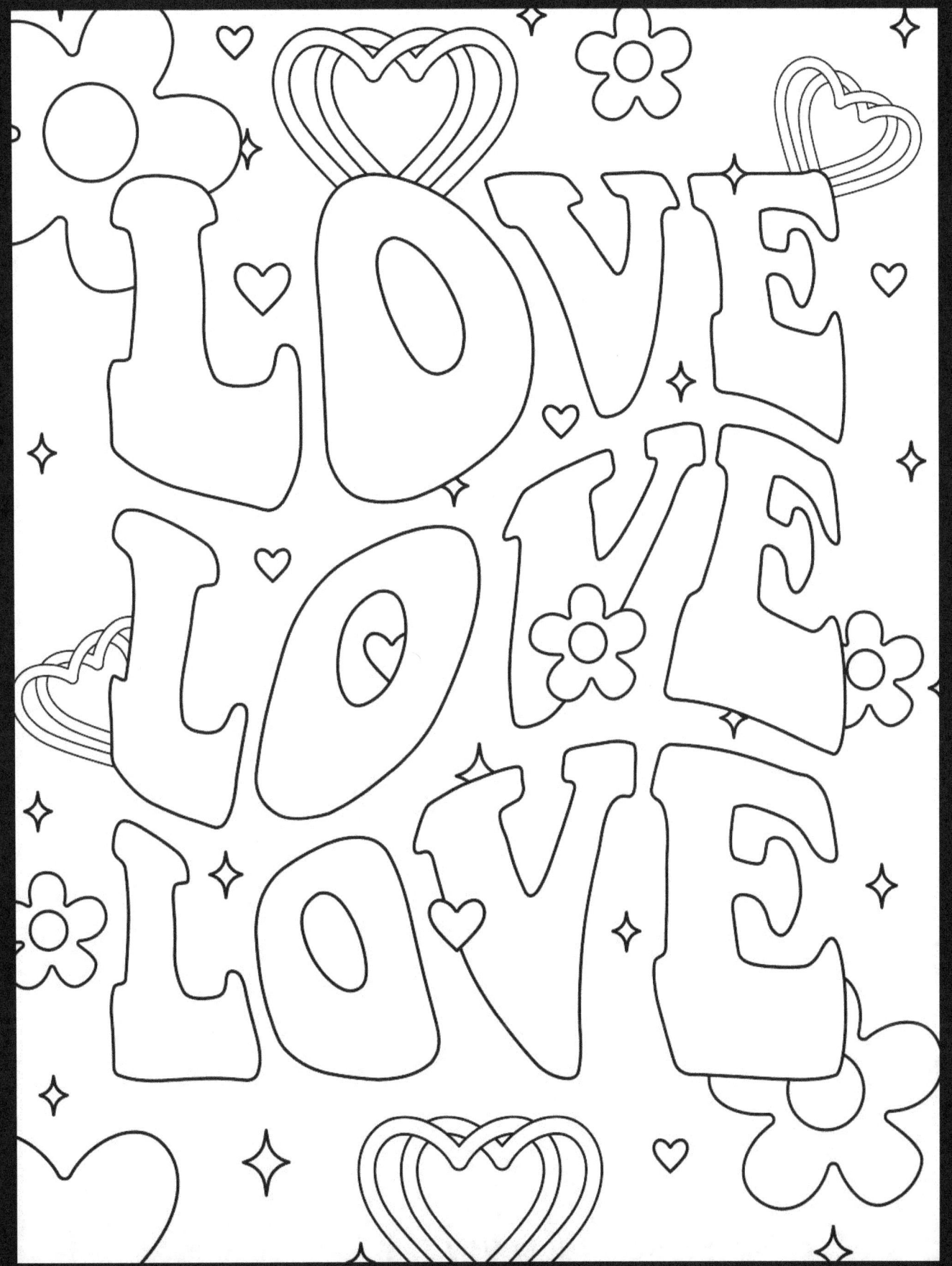

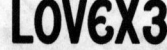

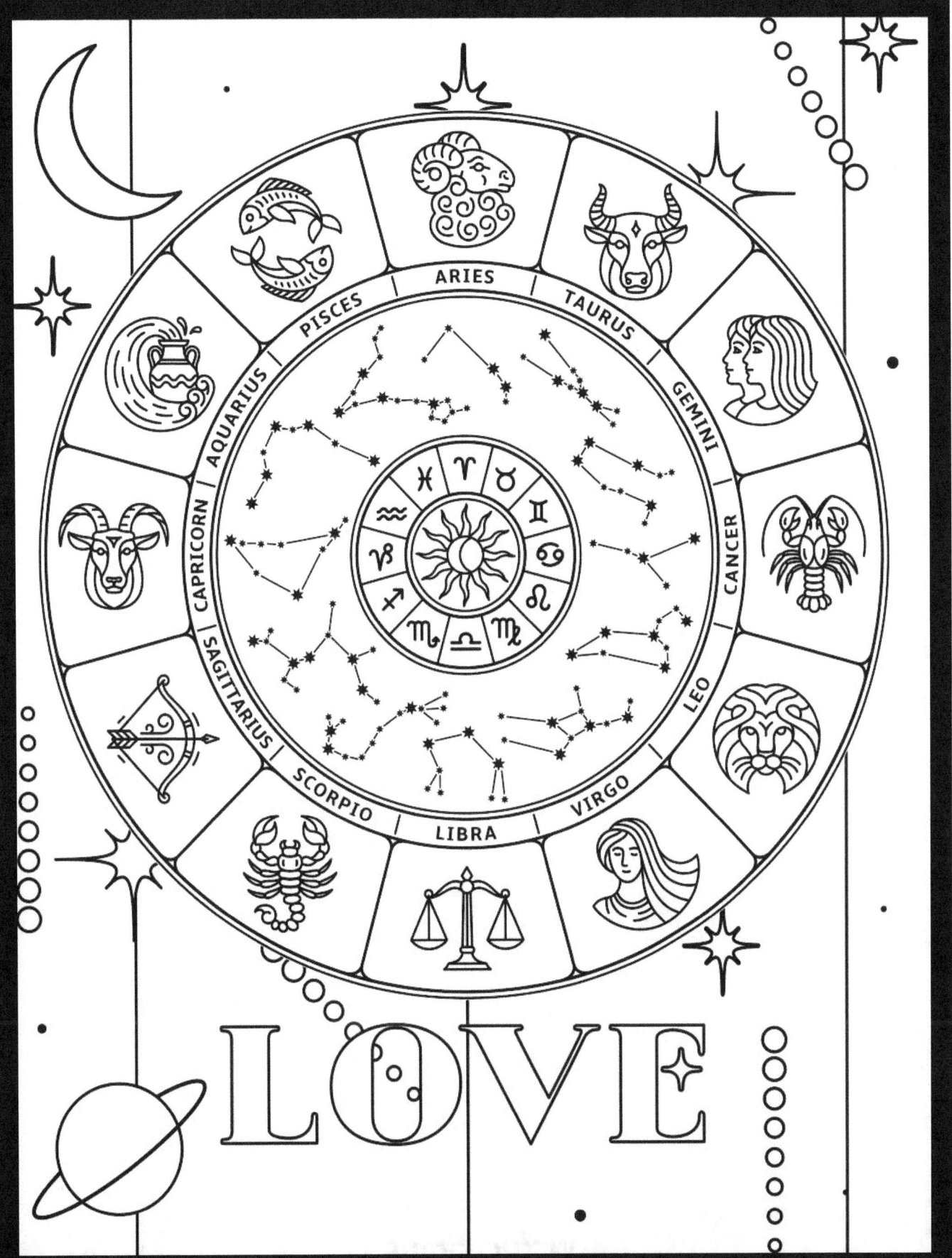

IN THE STARS

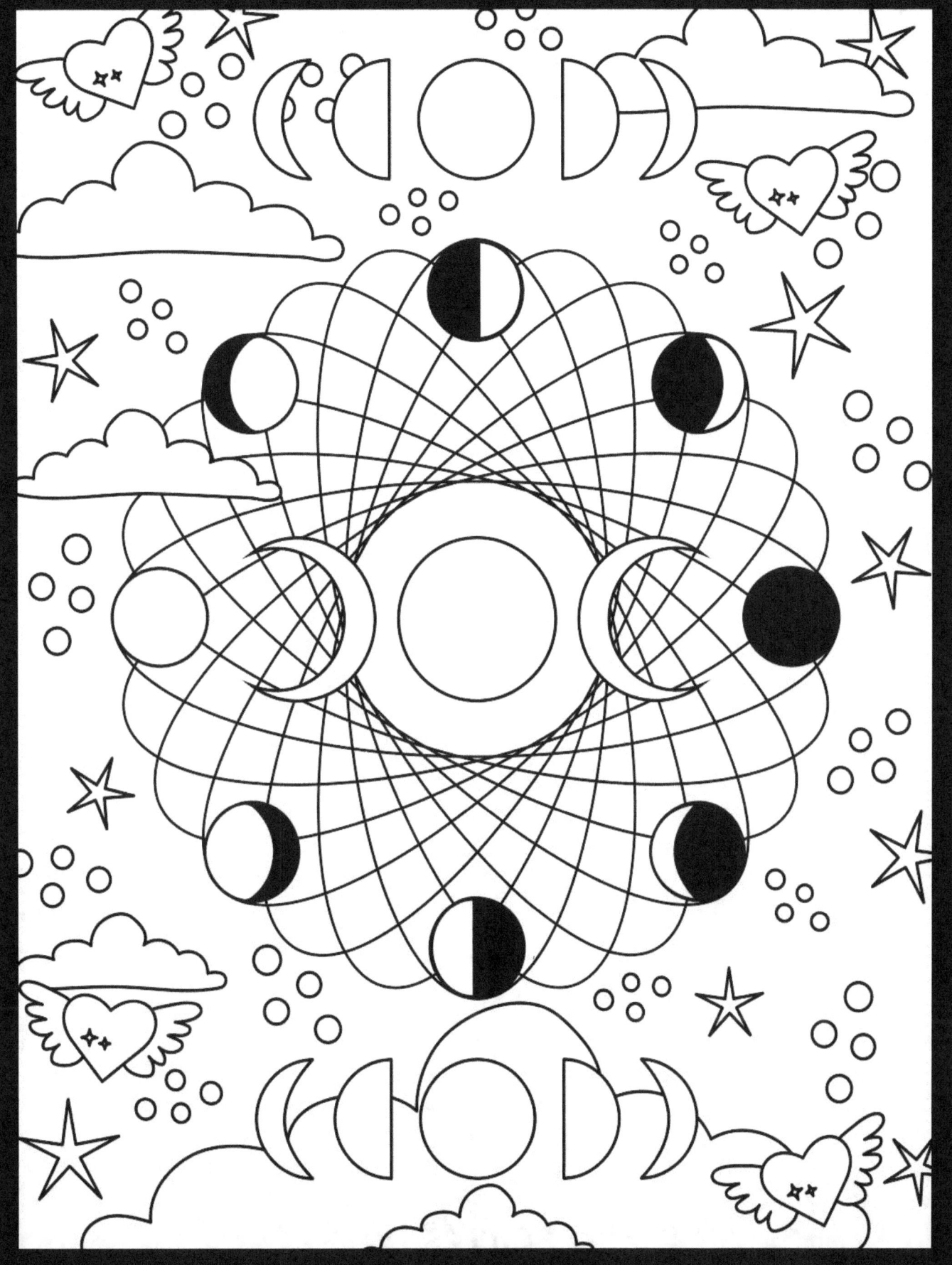

CYCLES

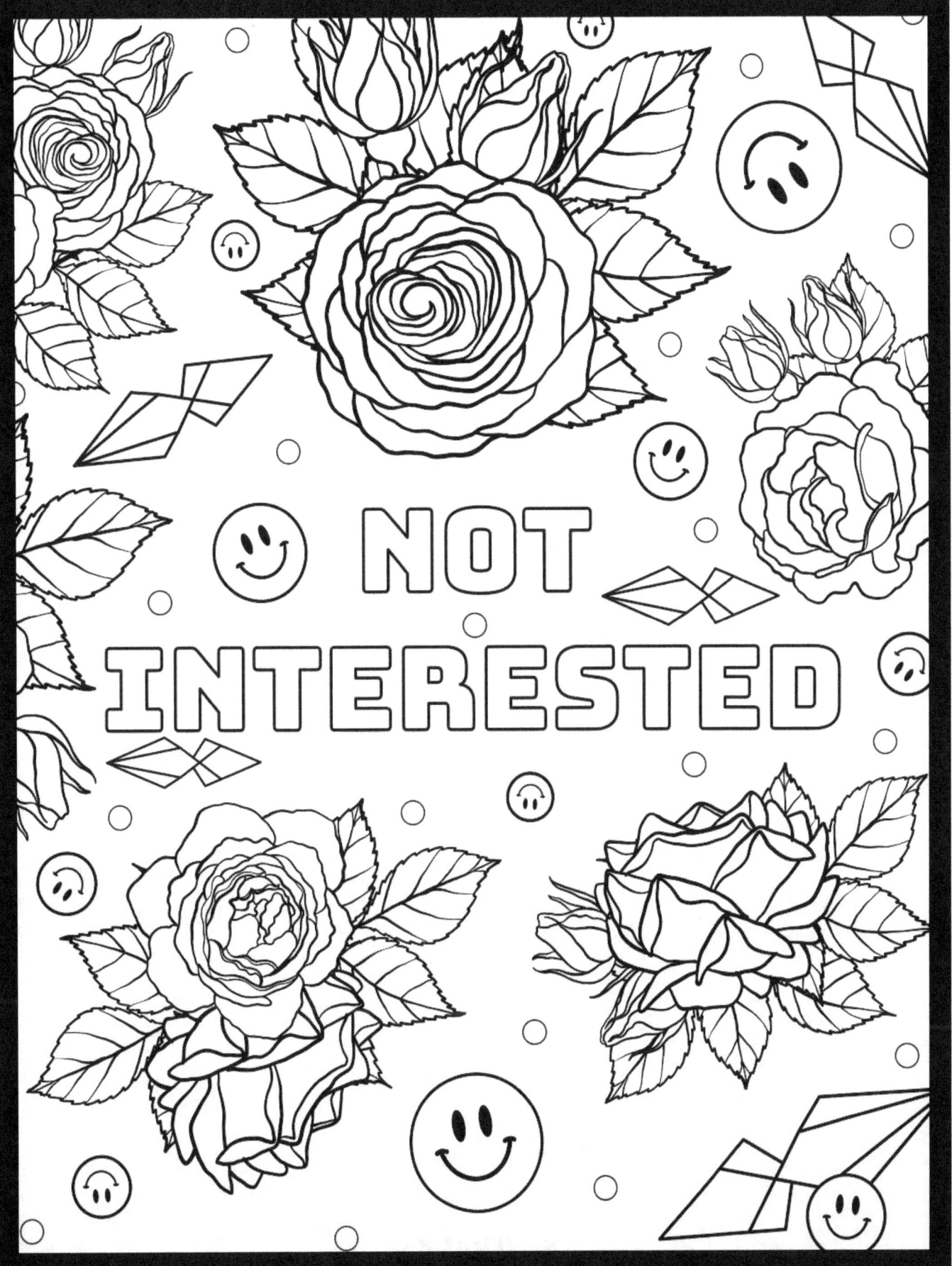

NO THANKS

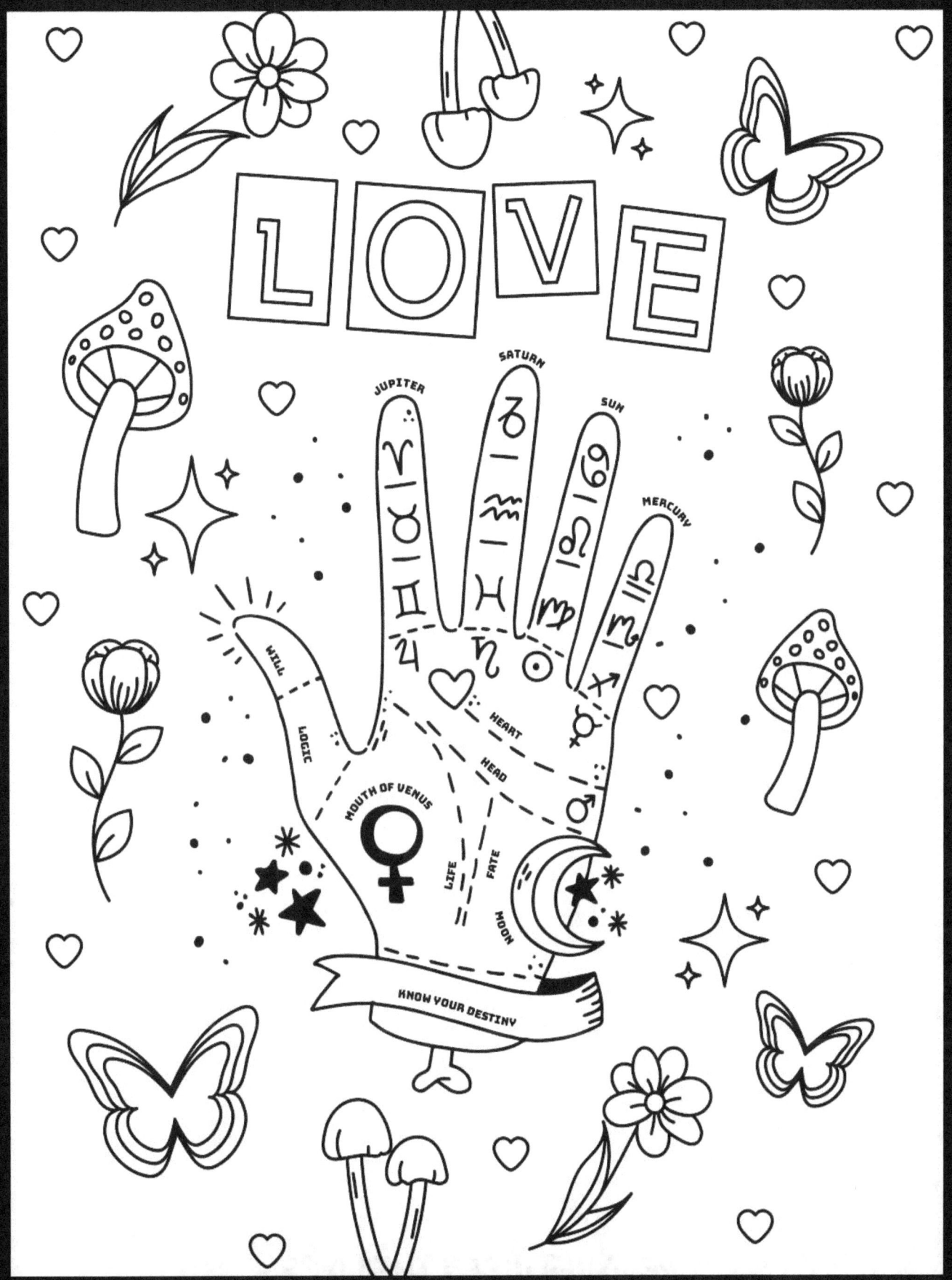

READ BETWEEN THE LINES

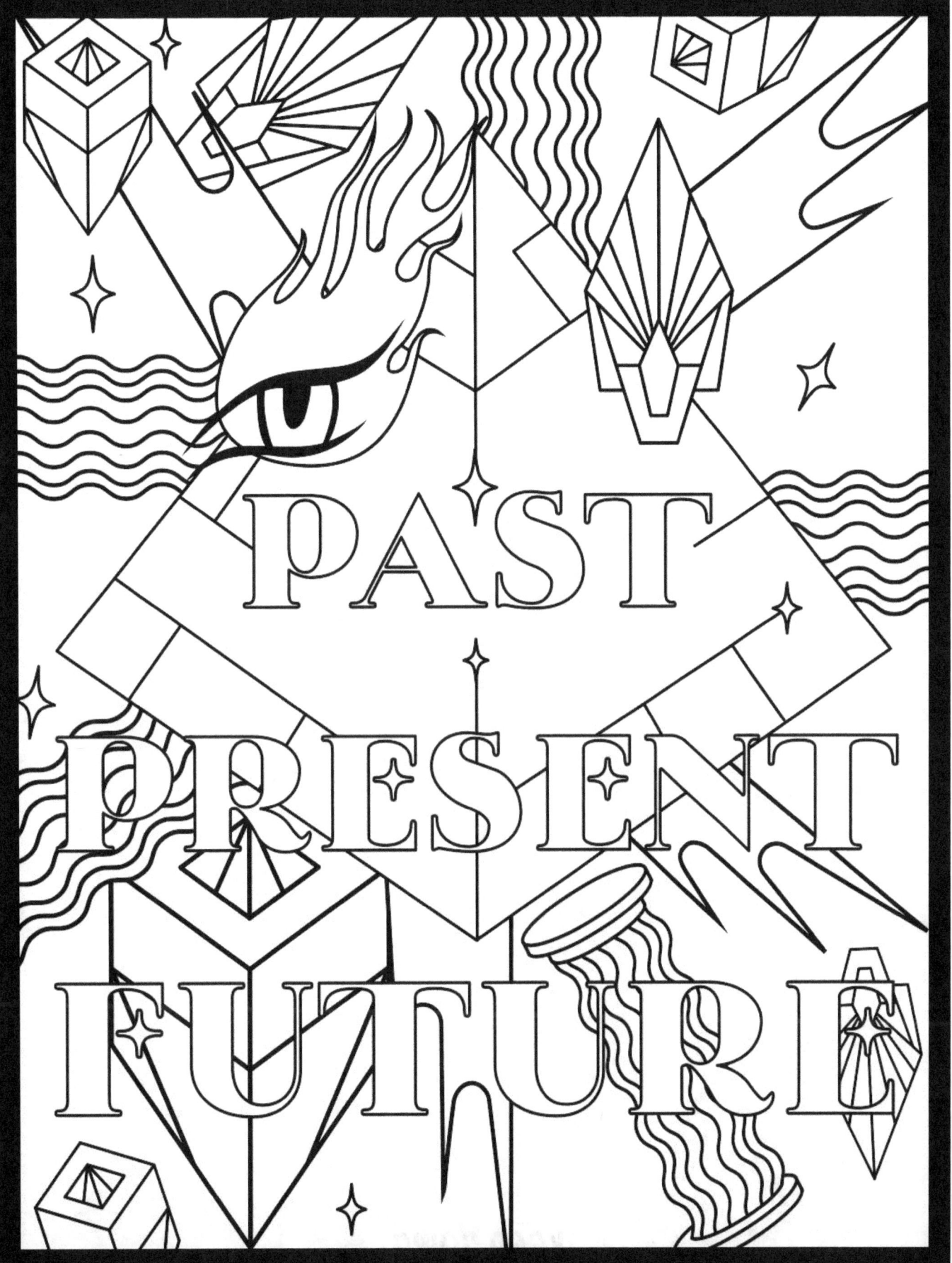

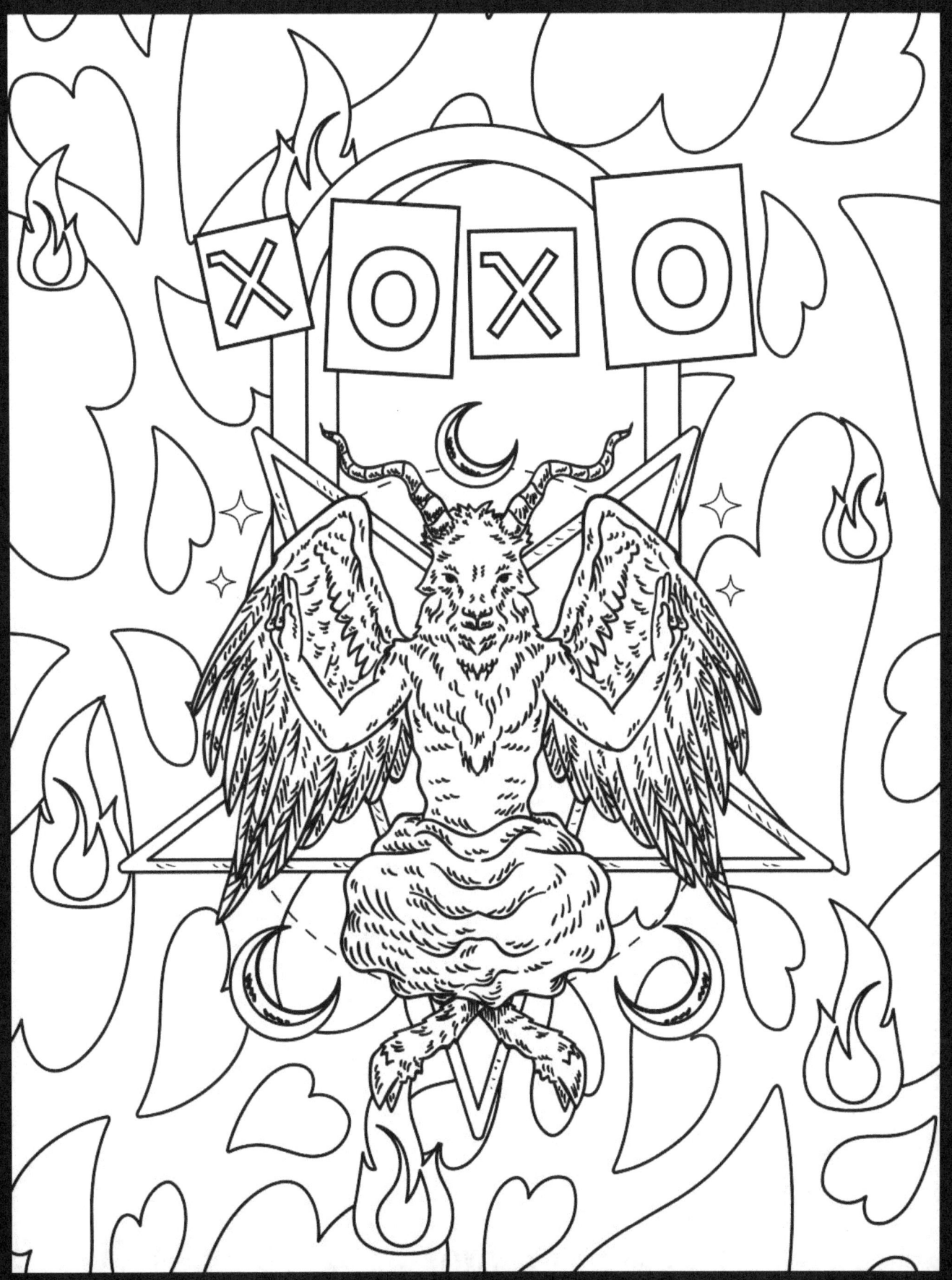

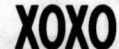

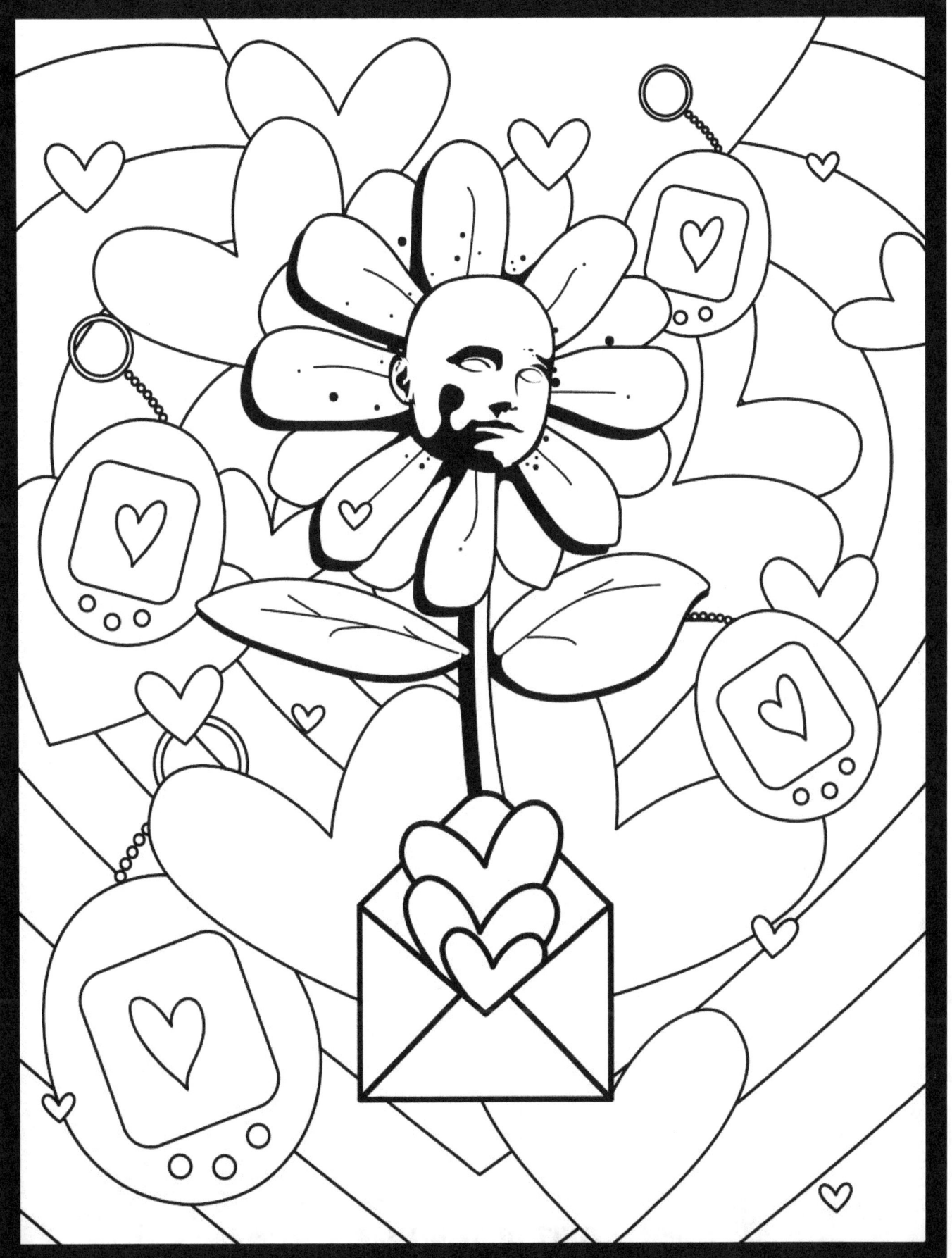

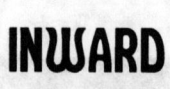

INWARD

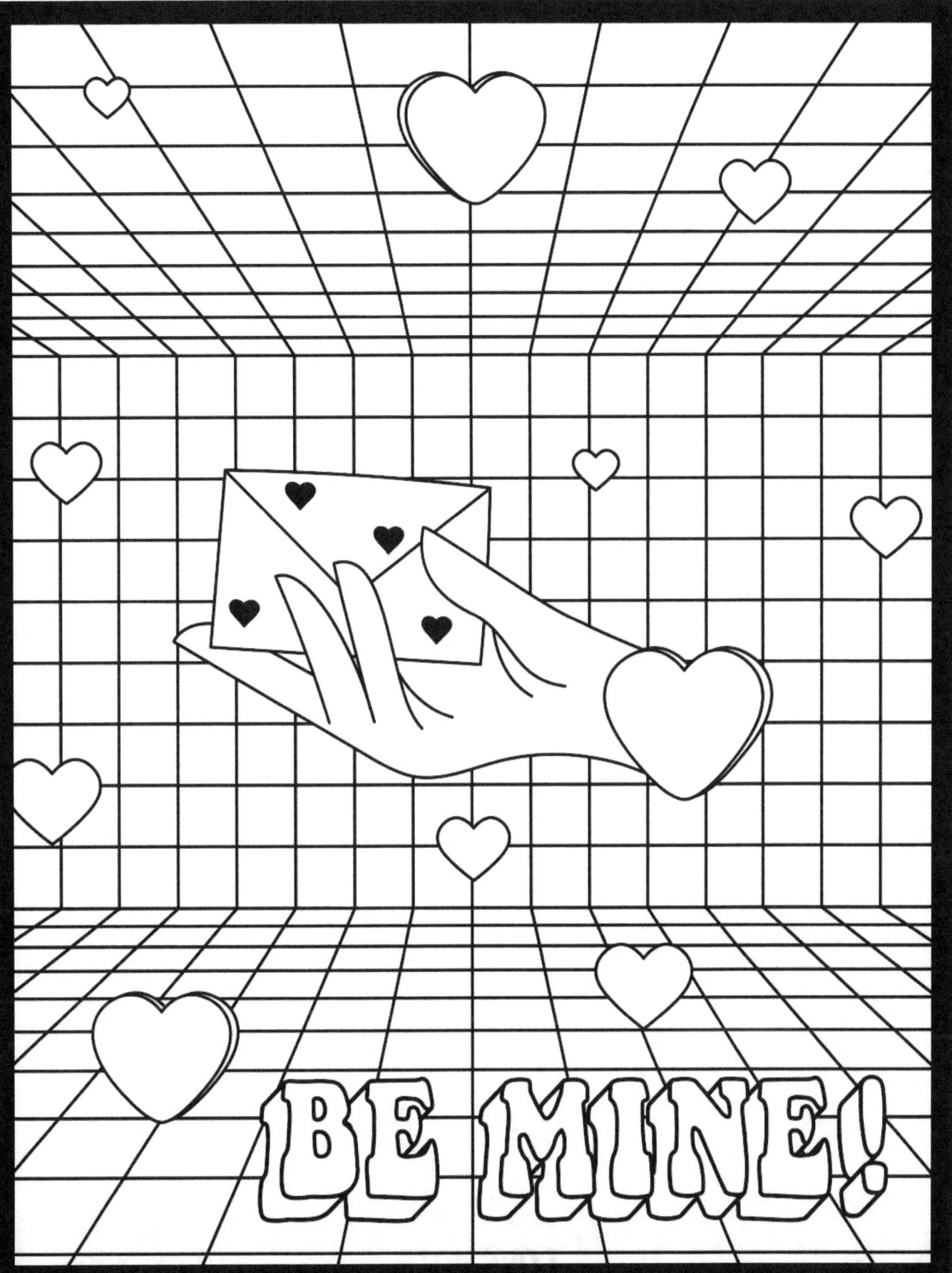

LOVE NOTE

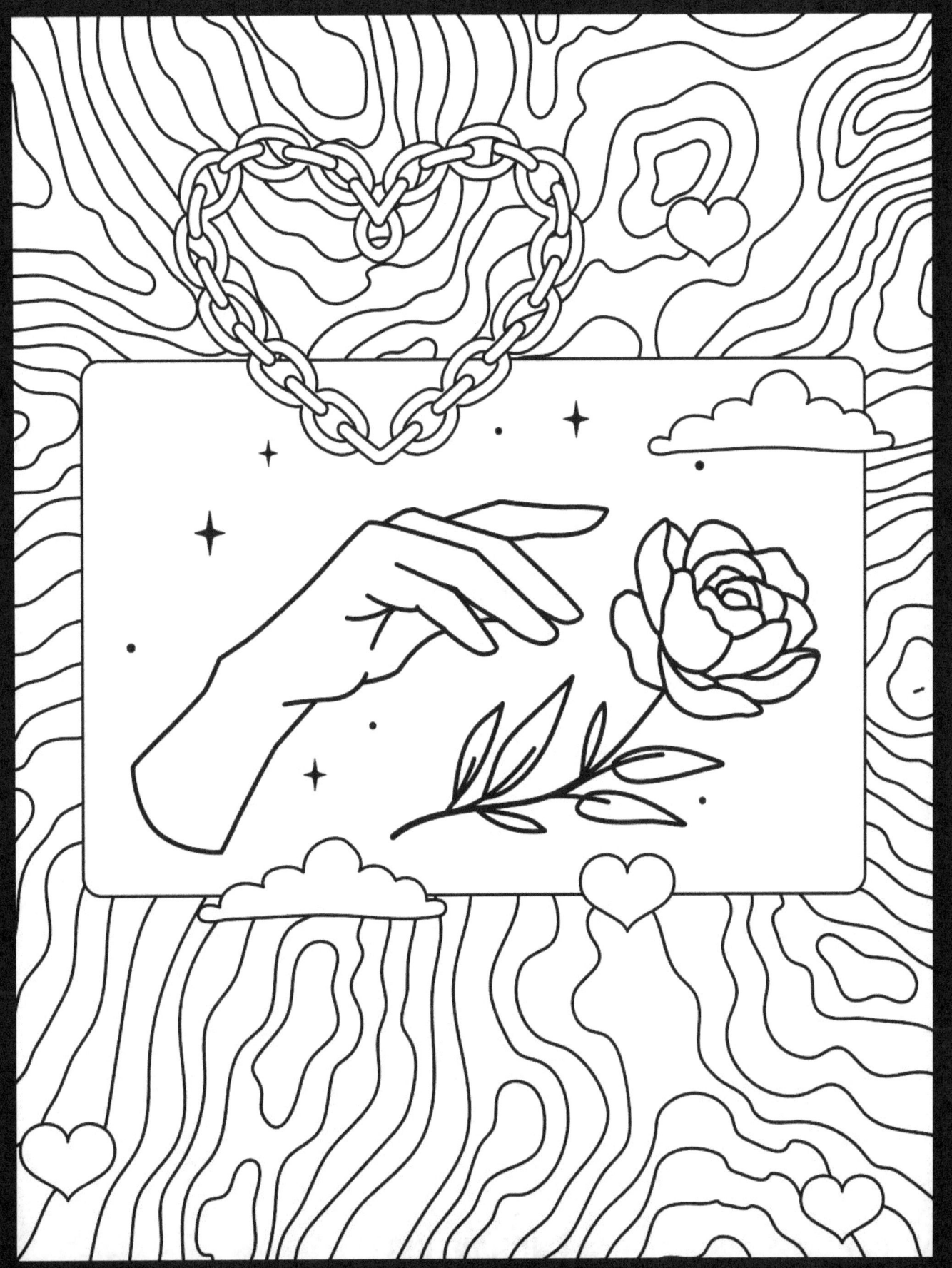

ENCHANTING

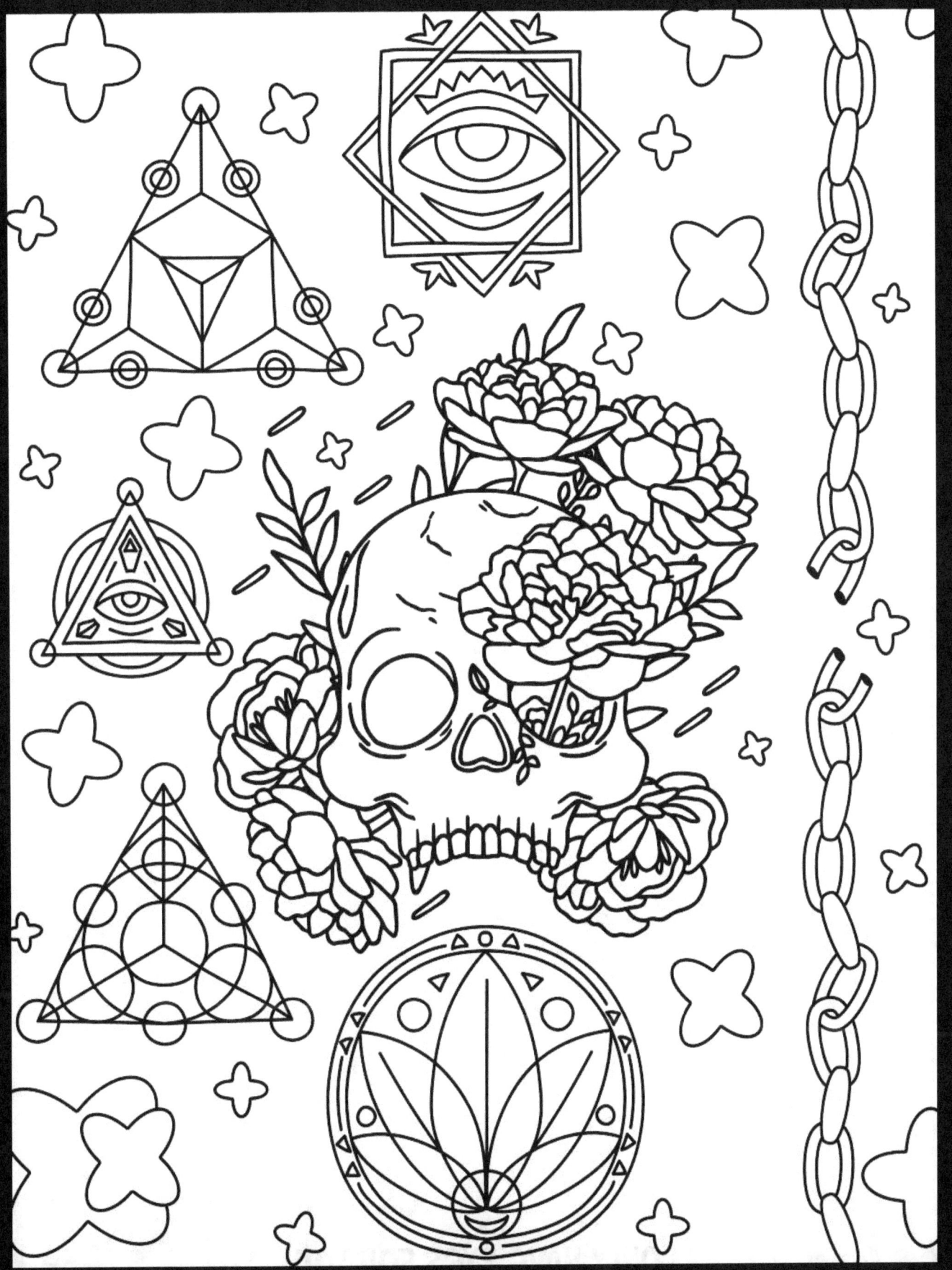

ONLY HAVE EYES FOR YOU

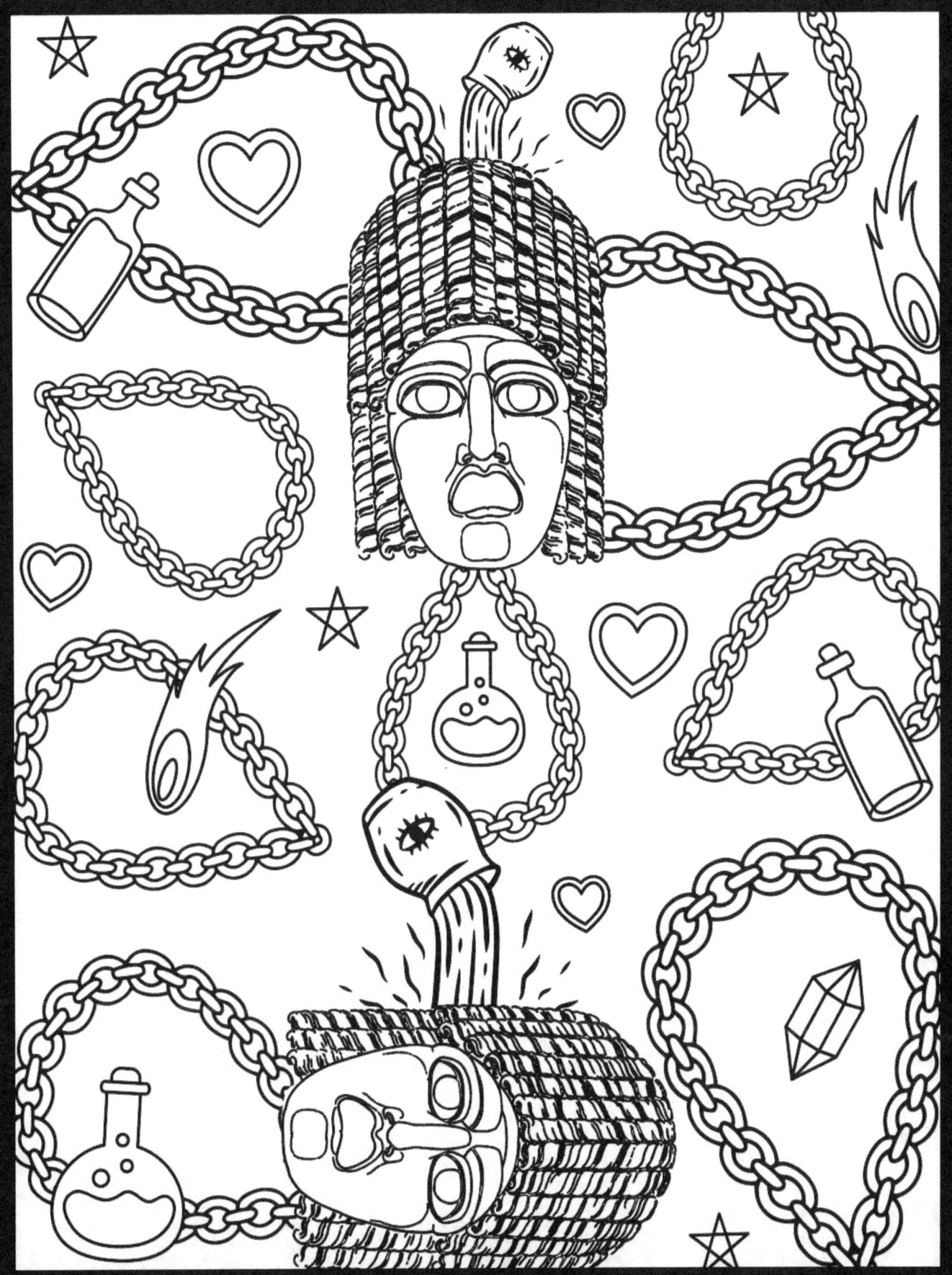

SPILL

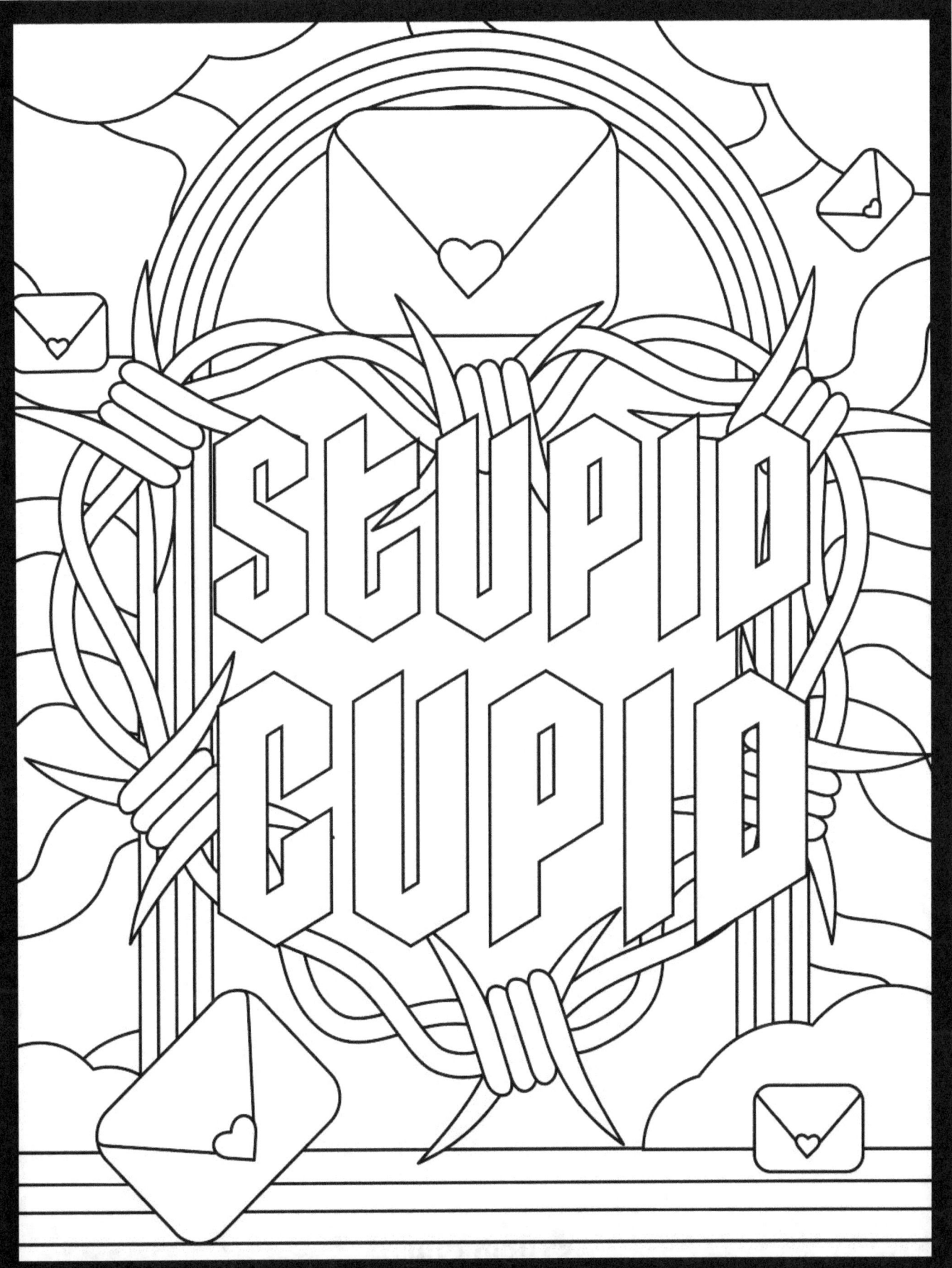

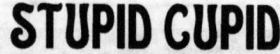

STUPID CUPID

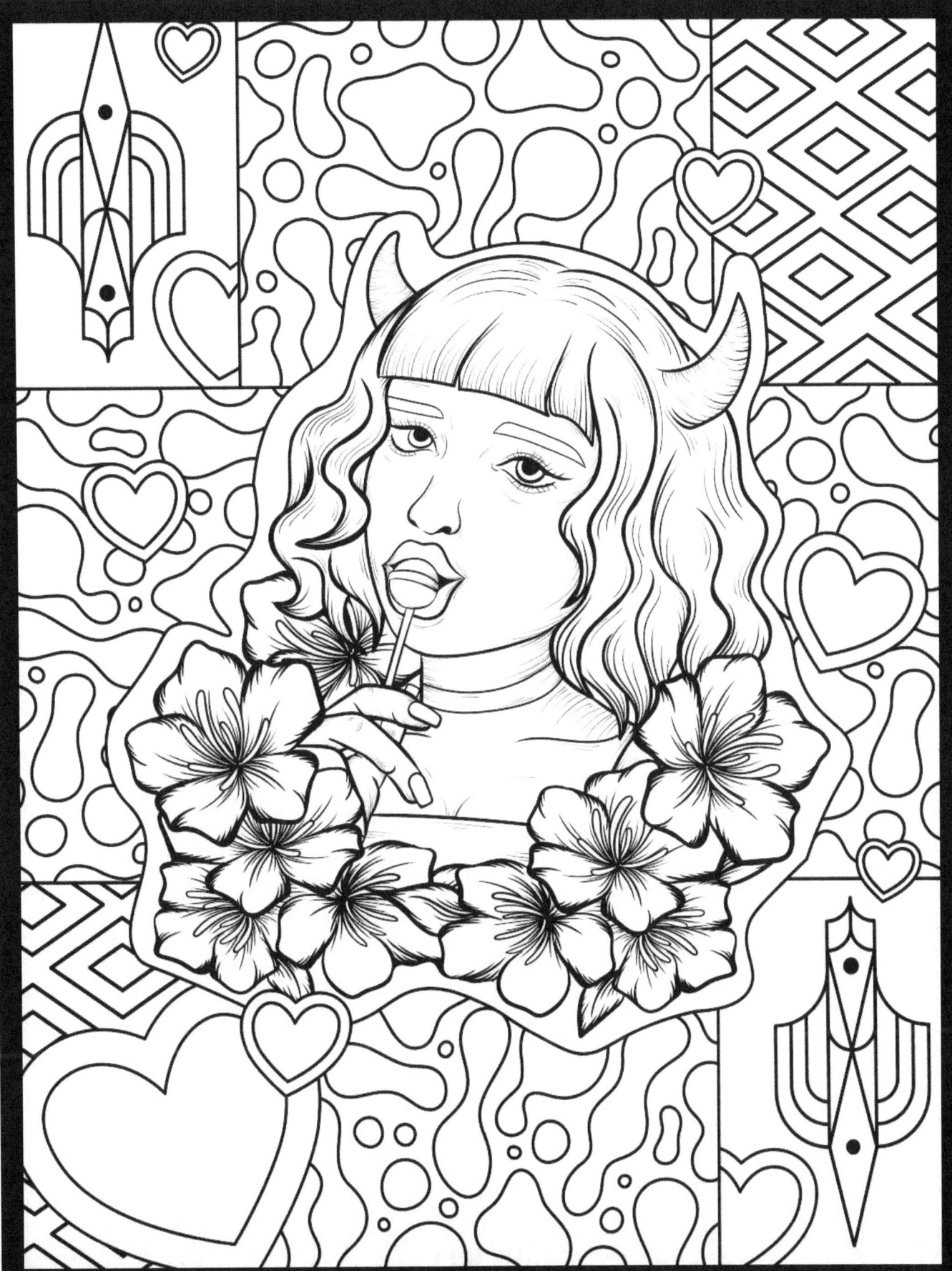

SUCK IT

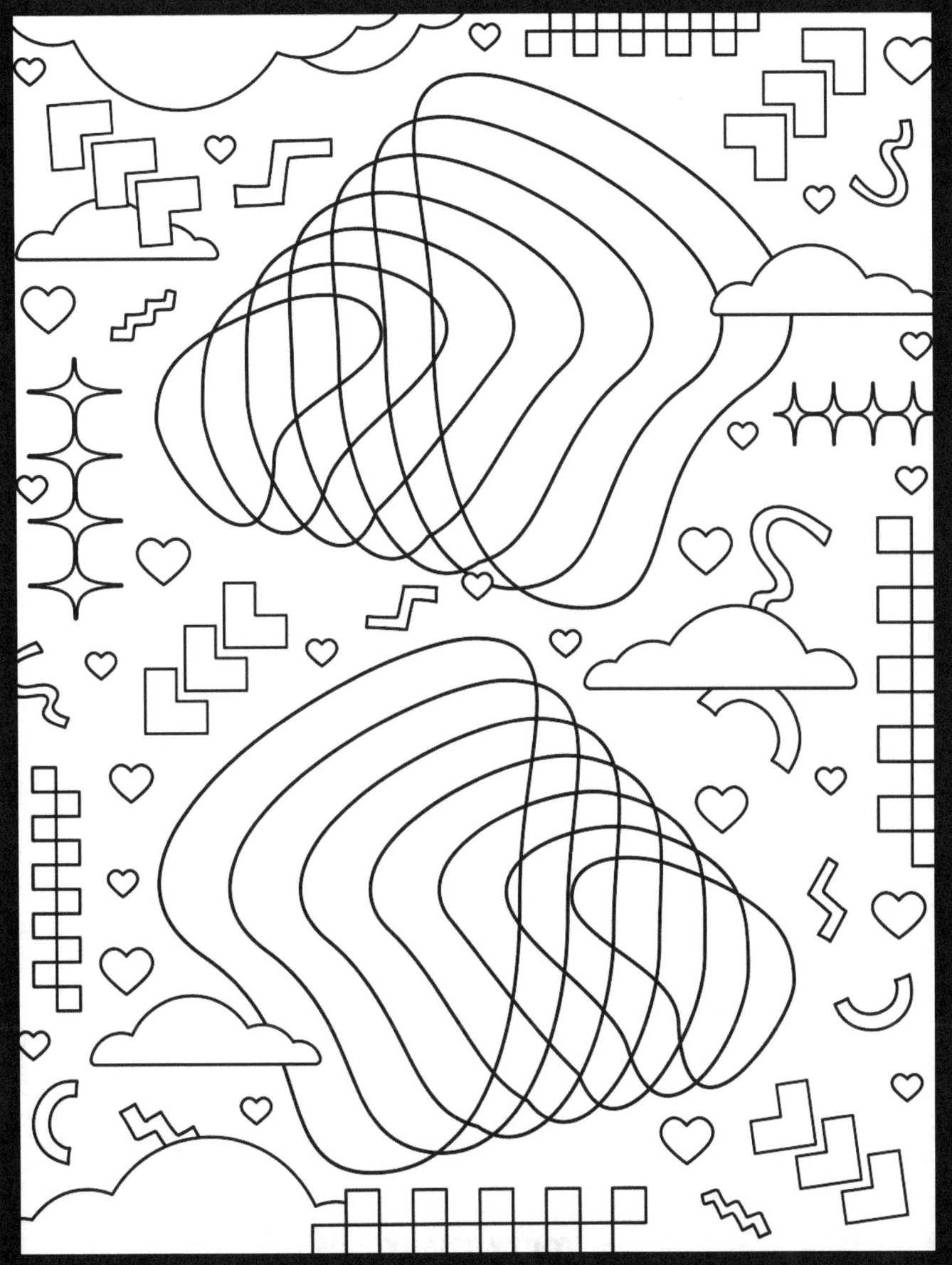

TOPSY TURVY

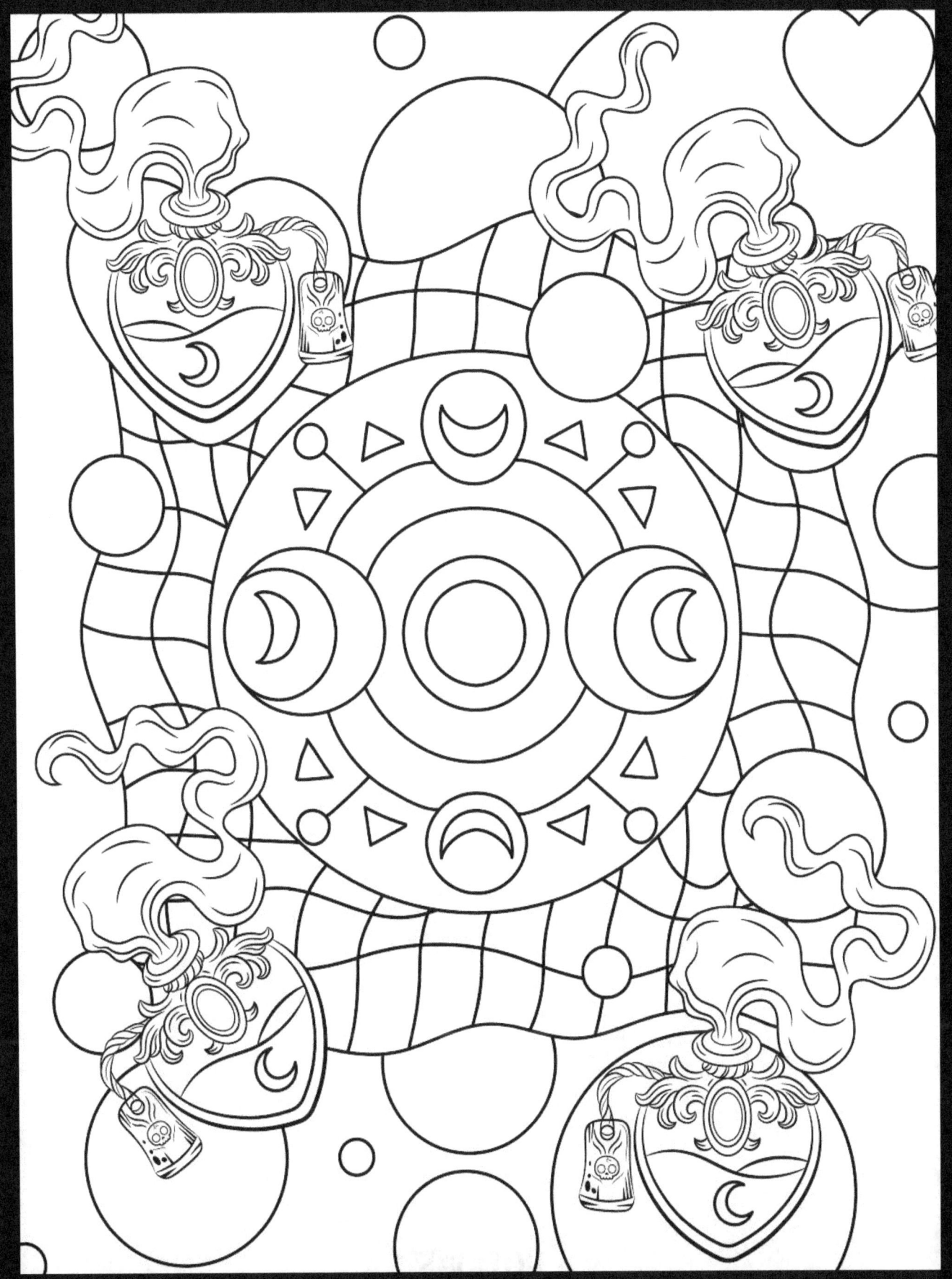

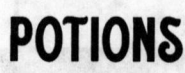
POTIONS

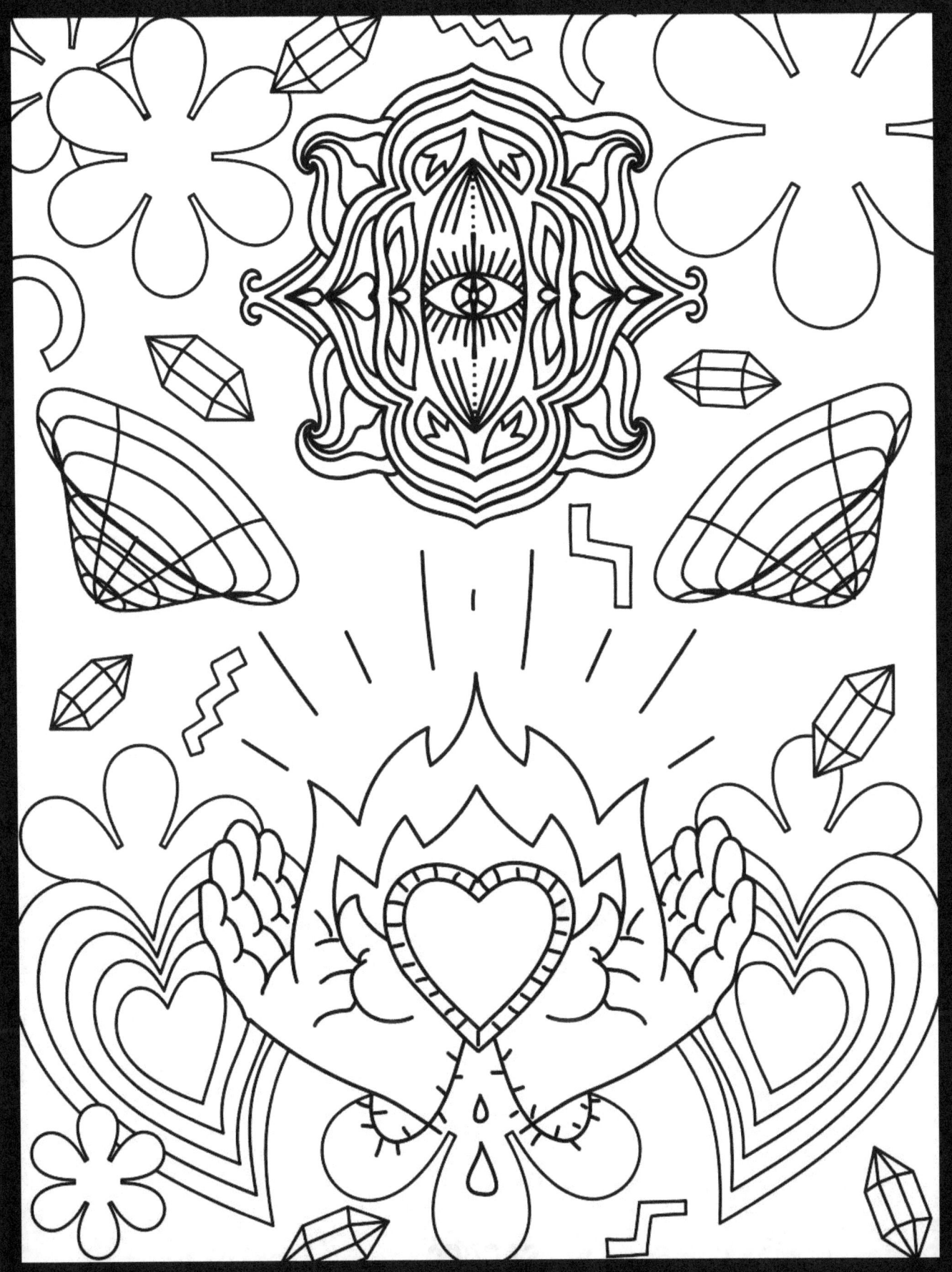

SACRED

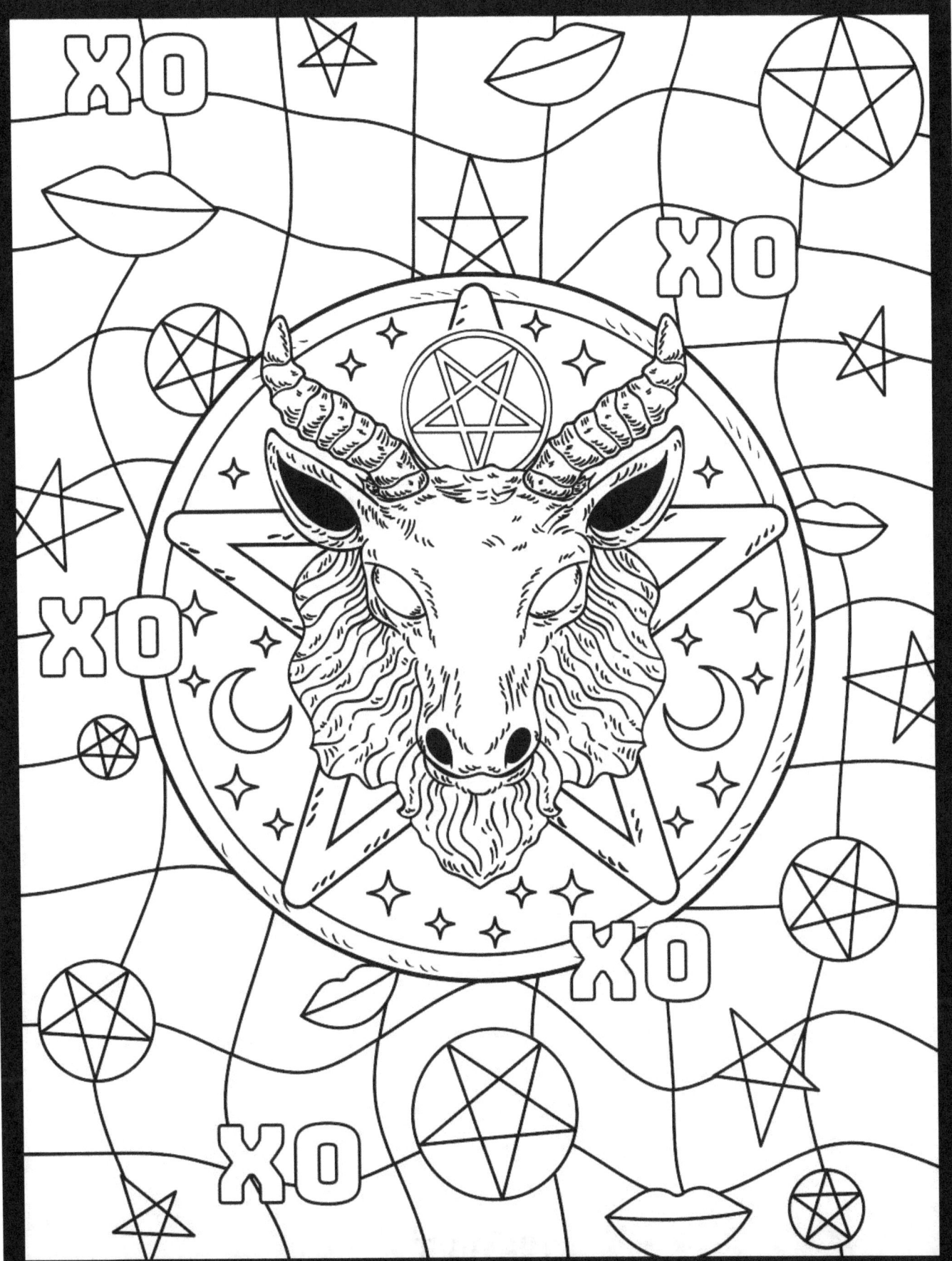

THE GOAT

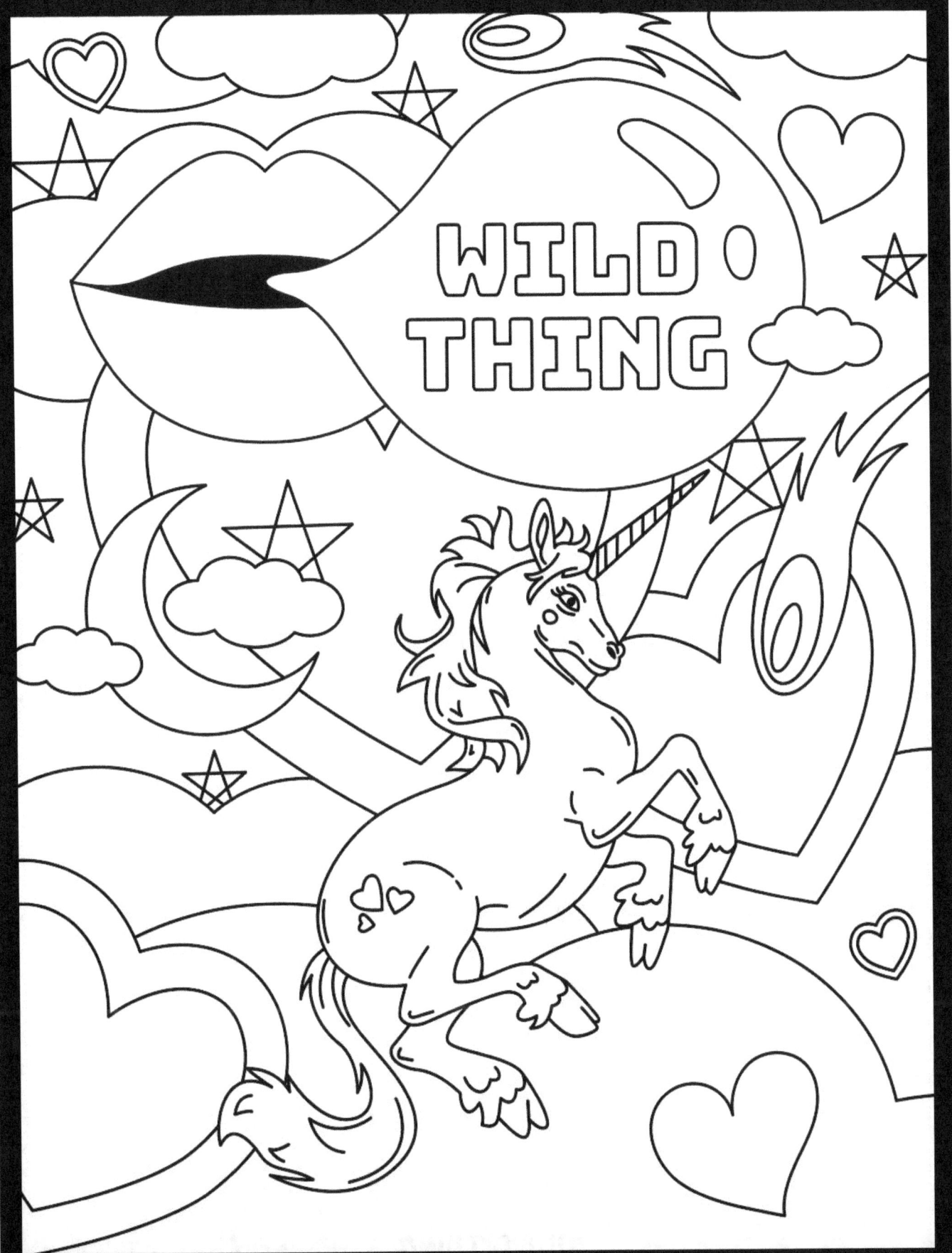

WILD THING

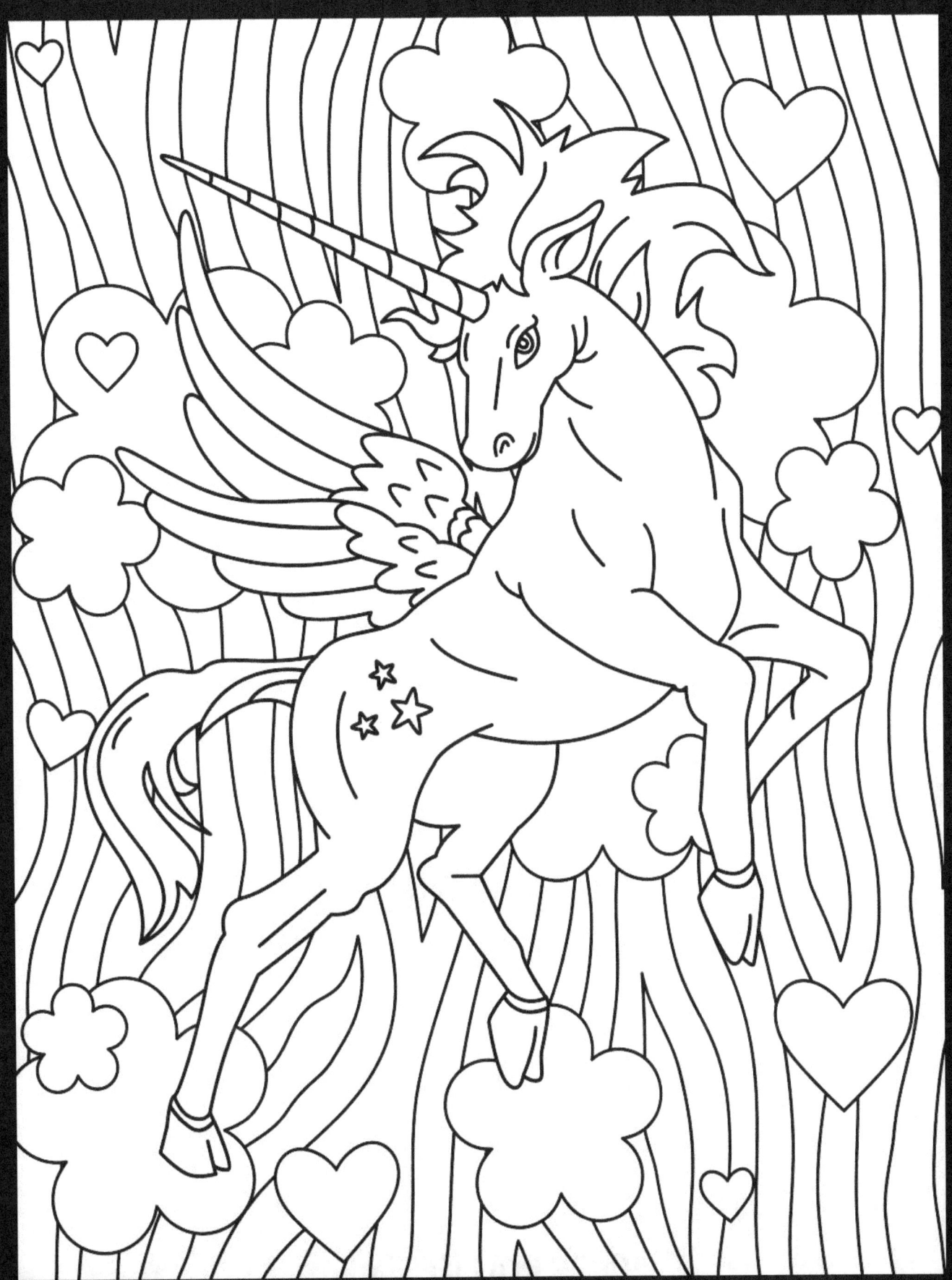

ONCE IN A LIFETIME

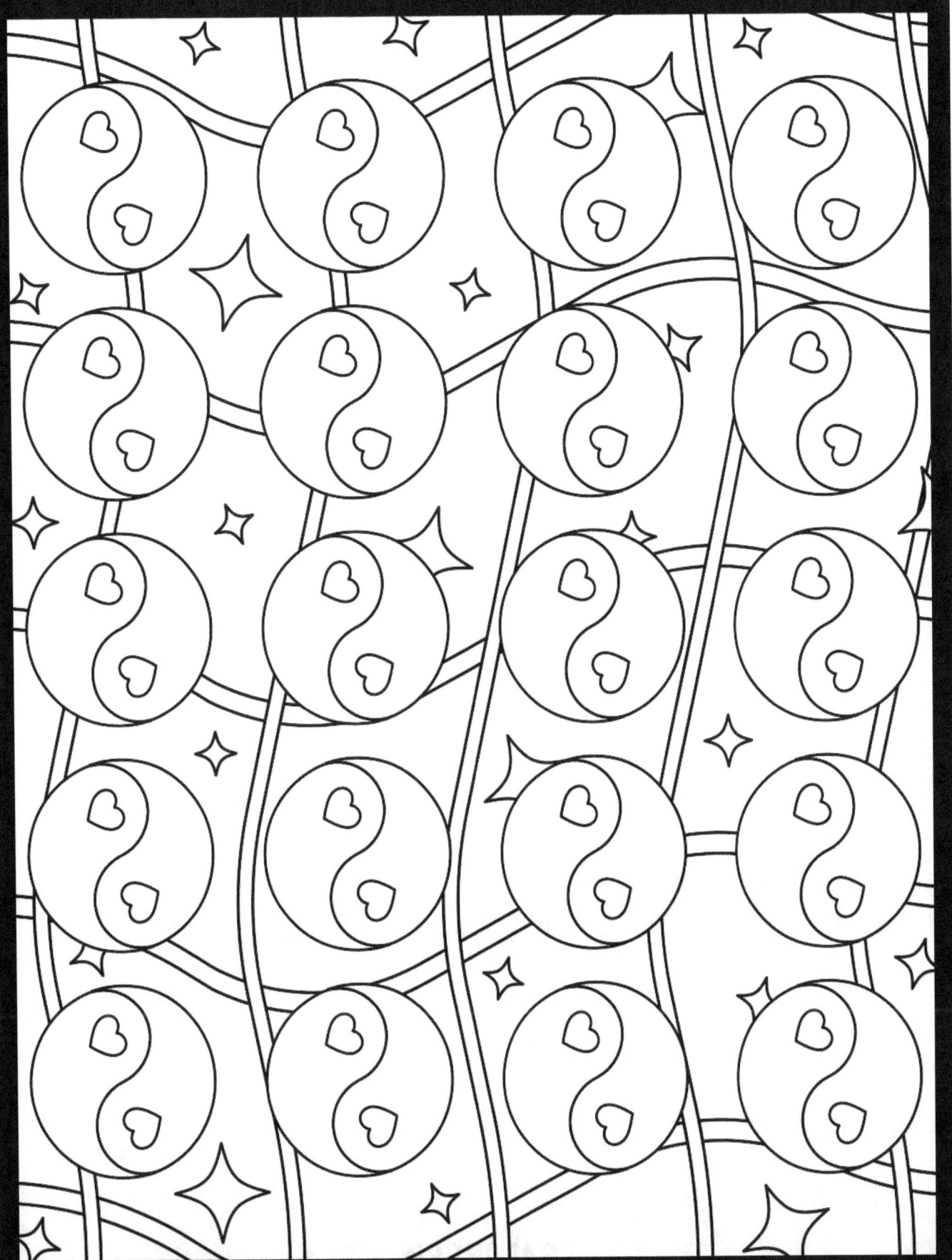

BALANCED

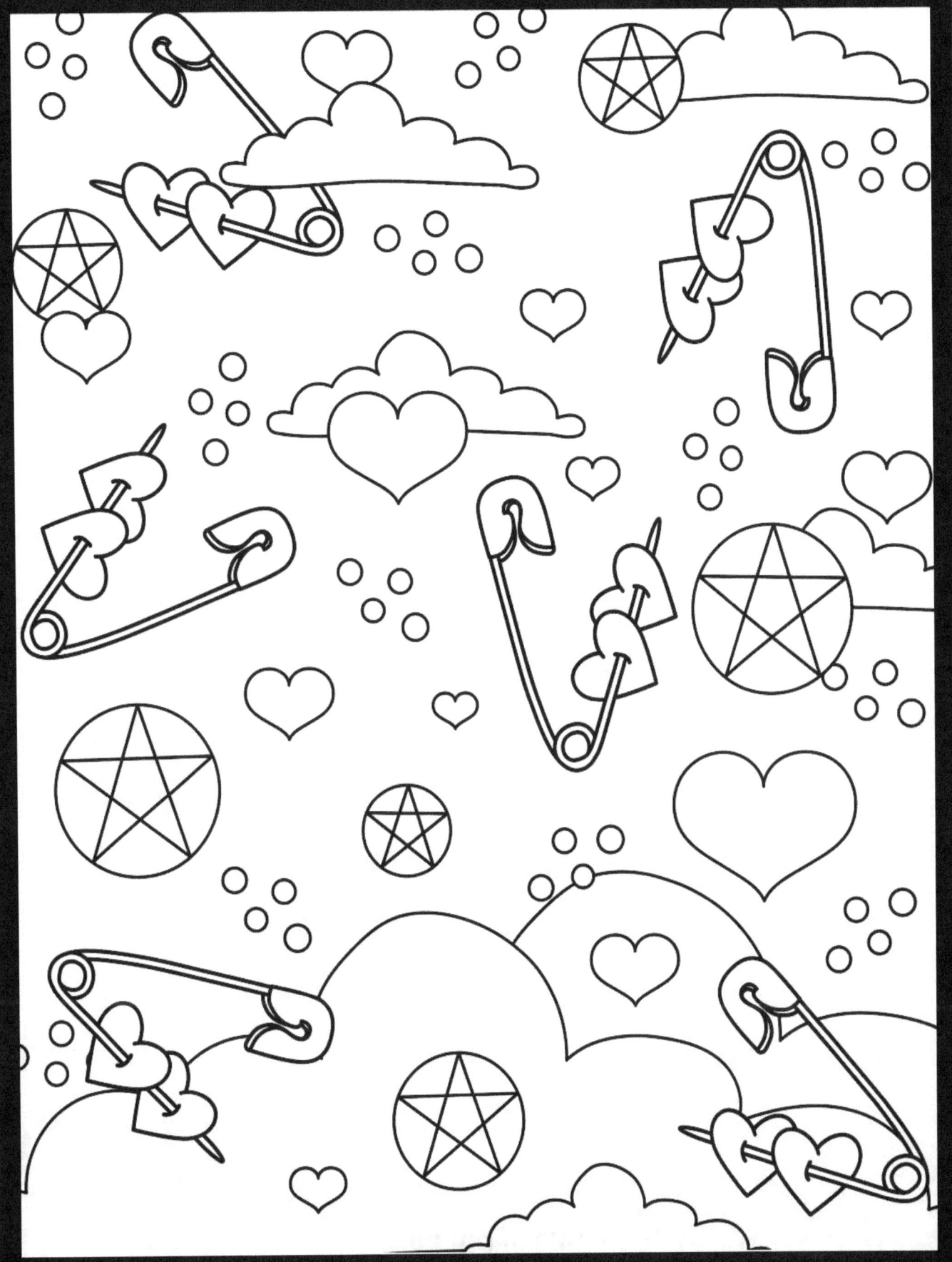

PUT A PIN IN IT

www.ingramcontent.com/pod-product-compliance
Lightning Source LLC
Chambersburg PA
CBHW080842220526
45467CB00008B/2362